Amplified Heart

An Emotional Discography

Bryn Gribben

For my mother and my first musical memory, in which morning has always broken like the first morning

For Rick—Same. Always.

And to all the girls and boys and Willie Nelson songs I've loved before

ISBN 978-1-7342621-9-3
Edited by Katherine Anderson
Cover design by Carmen Woodson

Printed in the United States of America

Otherwords Press
www.otherwordspress.net

Playlist One

Break-Up Songs and Burning: Music of Pain and Loss

You Know Something Is Happening but You Don't Know What It Is
> Bob Dylan, *"Ballad of a Thin Man"*

Searching for Lila Moore
> Bob Dylan, *"Tangled Up in Blue"*

I Don't Enjoy the Silence
> Depeche Mode, *"Enjoy the Silence"* / Bobby Bare, *"Skip a Rope"*

A Song with No Words for a Love that Could Not Speak Its Name or That of Any Other: A Fairytale of Sorts
> Duke Ellington, *"Fleurette Africaine"*

Where to Stand in the Room
> Joni Mitchell, *"All I Want"*

Divorce Closet
> The Magnetic Fields, *"Washington, D. C."*

Practice Room: Elliott and the Bands He Wouldn't (Couldn't) Leave

Jingle Bells: An Elegy
> Frank Sinatra version, *"Jingle Bells"*

Practice Room: "Big Love"

When Our Song Turns Back into Just Mine: The Break-Up Song
> Joni Mitchell, *"All I Want"*

Real Phone Number, Fake Name: On Anger, Music, and (Non) Intimacy
> Nicki Minaj, *"Super Bass"*

Playlist Two

Interstitial Music: Essays on In luence, Recovery and Protection

Message in a Bottle
> The Police, *"Message in a Bottle"*

Paint It Blacker: How I Came to Love the Rolling Stones
> The Rolling Stones, *"Complicated"*

There Goes the Fear: Sound and Vision
> Doves, *"There Goes the Fear"*

What to Save
> Kings of Convenience, *"I Don't Know What I Can Save You From"*

One Line: P. J. Harvey and the Cosmos
> P. J. Harvey, *"One Line"*

How Soon Is Now: Music and Fear
> Kishi Bashi, *"I Am the Antichrist to You"* and
> The Smiths, *"How Soon is Now"*

How 80s Music Set Me Up to Yearn and Fail and Survive
> Phil Collins/Marilyn Martin, *"Separate Lives," and others*

You Remind Me of the Babe: Labyrinths, Tegan and Sara, and Going
Nowhere with Love
> Teagan and Sara, *"Where Does the Good Go?*

Playlist Three

Just Burning: Songs of Joy, Divided

High School Orchestral Maneuvers in the Dark and in Broad
Daylight
> OMD, *"Sailing on the Seven Seas"*

Devo Made My Sister Cool
> Devo, *"Time Out for Fun"*

Patti of the World's Two Greatest Love Songs
> The Beatles, *"Something,"* and
> Eric Clapton, *"Layla"*

These Arms Were Mine: First Love is a Slow Dance that Goes On Forever
> Otis Redding, *"These Arms of Mine"*
> *(Hidden Track: The Summer We Knew We Were Young*
> Kate Wolf, *"Cornflower Blue")*

Everybody Got Their Something, or Pray Someone Steals Your College Music
Soon
> Nikka Costa, *"Everybody Got Their Something"*

Use Your Illusion: Import B-Sides

Ain't That Enough
> Teenage Fanclub *"Ain't That Enough"*

My Friend the Dreamer, the Muppet
> Eric Johnson, *"Forty Mile Town"* and
> Juliana Hatfield, *"Spin the Bottle"* No Deal with God
> Kate Bush, *"Running Up that Hill"*

Performance Art's a Kind of Love
> Animal Collective, *"Did You See the Words Today"*

*All art constantly aspires towards the condition of music. For while in all
other kinds of art it is possible to distinguish the mat-
ter from the form, and the understanding can always make this distinction, yet
it is the constant effort of art to obliterate it. That
the mere matter of a poem, for instance, its subject, namely, its given incidents
or situation — that the mere matter of a picture, the actual circumstances of
an event, the actual topography of a landscape — should be nothing without
the form, the spirit, of
the handling, that this form, this mode of handling, should be-come an end
in itself, should penetrate every part of the matter: this is what all art
constantly strives after, and achieves in different degrees.*

--Walter Pater, "The School of Giorgione"

Oh, I love you / when I forget about me.

–Joni Mitchell, "All I Want"

Preface

Burning Always with a Hard Gemlike Flame, or Why All Art Aspires to the Condition of Music

My heart is not private. It is, proverbially, on my sleeve, and I keep the cuffs rolled down, so you can have access to it. That moment when John Cusack holds up the boom box and blares Peter Gabriel under Ione Skye's window? I brought a whole trio of friends to sing "Unchained Melody" outside a high school boyfriend's house. This has not always been smart. Once, I walked into a lover's art show to find my own face floating up from a collage of my emails to him, whole and desperate emails pasted amidst flattened, smudged cocktail umbrellas.

So, yes—this has not always been smart. But it has been what I've done.

My relationships, romantic or platonic, occupy me like a social revolution, but the change I achieve isn't always clear. It's as if I started using the intellectual power I once had now for the mere purpose of understanding why someone doesn't call after two days. But I'm well-known among friends as the one to enlist, when you need to unpack a heart break. As Oscar Wilde famously once said , "At times, I feel as if I'd put all of my genius into my personality and, sadly, only my talent into my art."

I read Wilde as a senior in college, but more importantly, I read *Studies of the Renaissance* by Wilde's mentor, Walter Pater. I read him while drinking tea, lying on my loveseat, where I'd had tea and made out with so many, and suddenly, I felt my whole being come into focus. Pater describes the very process of seeing as that—a process of impact upon impact—and concludes that the secret to genius is to discern, at all times, the most private qualities of one's experiences—to revel in the sensual process of experience—rather than glean the "fruits of experience," the analysis that benefits you later. "To burn always with this hard, gemlike flame, to maintain this ecstasy, is success in life," he says.

I don't think I understood all of it, really. But that was the point for

Pater—if you felt it, you understood it. I remember reading and re-reading sentences, his writing itself, that hard, gemlike phrase, a new and exquisite reading experience, like drinking perfume or wrapping oneself in thick velvet. The fusion of "burning" with "hard" and "gemlike"—the geological solidness with the sparkling of the gem . . . that image stood out, as something rare and separate from my college reading, a gem on its own, not a bead on a necklace. I heard, in the way I needed to hear it, the voice of someone else who understood how deeply marvelous I thought life was, how hot and comforting this tea, this couch, a soft hand to one's face.

I burst inside, my own mind a disco ball illuminated with pleasure that this timid man, an Oxford tutor who preferred to entertain privately, found words for what I felt certain described each of the moments I made in this world. "All art," he also said, "aspires to the condition of music." A burning and musical vanishing, experience on the air.

I burned all through my twenties when it's most crucial to do so. I burned, got burned, and sparkled and drank and tasted and kissed and bought plane tickets too expensive for me. I burned into my mid-30's and read as much Pater as I could, but nothing's ever been as good as the gem line, as effective at exciting that part of me that knows how important it is for me to know that burning is true, that living so intensely is the only real way to live.

But around 40, I began thinking more about other lines later in Pater's con-clusion—this line, actually: "Not to discriminate in every moment some pas-sionate attitude in those about us, and in the very brilliancy of their gifts some tragic dividing of forces on their ways, is, on this short day of frost and sun, to sleep before evening." And I think of this line because it is often raining in Seattle, and it is cold, and dark, and because I worry, more often than not, that I am sleeping and not burning. I get overwhelmed by the tragedy of the "trag-ic dividing of forces on their way." I wonder if the music is growing faint.

I feel myself reaching painfully out to hold onto those things that are leaving, that exceed my reach. Or, worse, I simply look at the frost and sun and cannot discern why I should reach at all. And yet, I am not

2

sleeping—I lay awake at night, most nights, worrying about how to be that gemlike flame. Yet really, what I worry about most is why I don't want to want more. I try to tell myself to let go of wanting more—of being more productive as a writer or as a scholar or as anything else I want to be, partially—letting go of anxiety about producing is exactly what Pater means when he says "it is not the fruit of experience, but experience itself is the end." I want to believe that I am still burning, but burning in ways that illuminate small-er things, tinier gems—that I am discovering, at this time of life, the crys-talline structures of an atom, instead of the crystal palace of my twenties. To really, truly live Pater, I am going to have to walk through these fires, even as I am the flame itself, and pray that, in all that heat, something fuses that can fuel me. Pater says "only to be sure it is passion" that drives me to experience, and that those experiences produce a "quickened, multiplied consciousness." I am giving myself all that I can, but I wonder what he told himself in the middle of the night, and what it felt like when his flame was low.

And this is where the music comes back in.

I decided to invite it back in, one song at a time. For one month, in May 2013, I started a Facebook project on one theme: "Music Intro-duced to Me by Other People that Makes Up for the Loss of My Close-ness to Them." Each Facebook status update was dedicated to one song and one person. At the end of May, I needed more than thirty-one days.

And so, I kept writing. And others read what I wrote. I'd run into an ac-quaintance in a bar and get bombarded by questions about what I was writing next, how they saved my posts for the end of the day, as a treat. How they sometimes felt better after reading them. I remembered what writing is really about, which is simply this: listening better to myself and sharing that "better" with others.

3

And maybe the worst.

But what I also found was how much I had not noticed in my burning: how much love, how much intention. And how much music. Always, always music.

I want this book to reflect the fleeting quality of music as experience, what Pater describes as the "movement, with the passage and dissolution of impressions, images, sensations, that analysis leaves off—that continual vanishing away, that strange, perpetual weaving and unweaving of ourselves." Therefore, this book is organized in terms of playlists on a theme, with two box sets of longer, multi-sectioned essays, a hidden track, an EP, a B-sides import, and a remixed conclusion. You can read around within it, shuffle the pages to find the tone that sings to you in your own moment. Or you can play this album and watch a woman try to sing herself back into burning.

Playlist One

Break-Up Songs and Burning: Music of Pain and Loss

Bob Dylan,
"Ballad of a Thin Man"

Bob Dylan,
"Tangled Up in Blue"

Depeche Mode,
"Enjoy the Silence" / Bobby Bare, *"Skip a Rope"*

Duke Ellington,
"Fleurette Africaine"

Joni Mitchell,
"All I Want"

The Magnetic Fields,
"Washington, D. C."

Frank Sinatra version,
"Jingle Bells"

Joni Mitchell,
"All I Want"

Nicki Minaj,
"Super Bass"

You know you love him. You love everything, though: this pink house next to the college, college itself, the endless days with girlfriends, the funny boys who live downstairs, the ten-window bedroom you will share with a friend who is also in love that summer and therefore never home. You are bright and happy; you're learning guitar, your professors hug you, and even his mom hugged you on the spot. You are so full of love, and that is why you're laughing in this kitchen, dancing with him to "Ballad of a Thin Man," laughing and kissing his face and then, and then, you start to cry, are crying. So full of love, which is why you let him leave.

Ah, you've been with the professors and they've all liked your looks
With great lawyers you have discussed lepers and crooks You've been
through all of F. Scott Fitzgerald's books
You're very well-read, it's well-known

You are both laughing in the kitchen, running ice cubes down each other's faces. Kansas in June already so hot, your graduation yesterday. She has one year left and sublets this oddly pink Craftsman for the summer with the friends who know, even if you do not, you are in love with her. They know she is in love with you, and she knows she loves you too. Your mother also knows, why yesterday she threw her arms around this laughing girl sweaty with moving, tee-shirt stained with irises she's stolen from the college to decorate this home. Everyone knows but you because you are afraid to know.

You walk into the room with your pencil in your hand You see
somebody naked and you say, "Who is that man?" You try so hard
but you don't understand
Just what you will say when you get home

She's crying— you don't wonder why, just look at her and drown a little more, as you've done each week since January, when you all went to that wedding in Ohio. You all went in that van, and it was freezing, and she talked to you for hours, and when the van broke down, you both stayed up and talked some more, while everyone else slept. You talked about your God, and how you needed to share that with someone, knowing she did not. She knew it, too, but still she held her face up to yours in the darkness of the van's backseat. You didn't kiss her then, said out loud "I can't." You thought you understood yourself so well back then.

But now she takes you to her bedroom, sunlight screening all ten windows, pouring all of summer in its Sunday suit into that bed, keeping the future out for three more hours when you'll leave her and this town to see that other Godly woman, but there's so much light this must be God so you think what the hell and peel her tee shirt off of her, stop feeling like you're drowning and dive like an ocean creature no one's ever seen.

> You raise up your head and you ask, "Is this where it is?" And
> somebody points to you and says, "It's his"
> And you say, "What's mine?" and somebody else says,
>   "Well, what is?"
> And you say, "Oh my God, am I here all alone?"

You told him in March his eyes were brown suns on an olive sky: jagged coronas around black pupils, then moss green green green to white. And he kissed you finally because you'd gone out with someone else. All those months of talking, then a rush to spend the last nights in the twin beds of each other's rooms, the moonlight bright in your room, the future's darkness in his. You don't even have to think "I love him"— he's off to spend this week with a woman you don't know, someone who thinks that God is real. You don't—you're smarter than that, and besides, don't you really know if you love him set him free? You are so innocent, you baby; you think that saying's true.

You're both virgins still, by choice: you because you'd become absorbed completely, him—you think—because it's morally wrong, so you'll both stay that way for another year. For all you think you know, this nakedness is quite enough, a bed frame like an undivided cell. He runs his thumb over the crest of your bra, smooths a seam already smooth. He makes a joke about bows and arrows, pointing to the tiny ribbon bow on your white underpants and the arrow on the band of his. You babies. Babies all.

Now, you see this one-eyed midget shouting the word "Now" And you say, "For what reason?" and he says, "How"
And you say, "What does this mean?" and he screams back, "You're a cow! Give me some milk or else go home"

You ask her to visit that summer, think you can always be friends. She looks up at you and nods. You get into your car, turn to see her put her face into her hands, like the girl in the postcard you gave her for no reason. You drive away to see about this other girl, hope she's the right fit. You are unaware your skin is luminous with the love of this girl you're leaving, each kiss of hers a bread crumb leading you away from home and God.

You have many contacts among the lumberjacks
To get you facts when someone attacks your imagination

You walk back into the pink house, to the bedroom, lay your face down in the sweat and melted ice water and the salt of your own . You think you are so brave to have loved and lost—another cliché you think is real—but you haven't lost a thing yet, little fool. You are brave because his body's still infusing you, his voice an ocean in your ear. How real is any promise to be friends when you are lovers, lovers, lovers? It's like saying you'll strangle the moon.

And without further notice, he asks you how it feels
And he says, "Here is your throat back, thanks for the loan"

You fearful man, it takes you a month to know the God Girl isn't right but a year to tell your weeping girl, iris-stained and sunny, that each postcard, phone call, email said I love you love you love you. You tempt all the other gods with your insistence you're just friends, and they're go-

ing to have to punish you, turn you to stone.

You foolish girl, you should have pulled him into your body, run after the car and said you didn't understand, that the talking meant the loving, that you don't want to be noble or him to be "free." Your poetry is lovely, but you will cut off all your hair in grief, sending him a foot of it in an envelope marked "friend."

There ought to be a law against you comin' around

You lose each other in your honor, forcing the fit of friendship on a glowing, pulsing thing. What you think is wisdom robs you both of love for years. This is wasting the youth upon the young: they leave love to show they can. You grow up and know none of it made sense, especially what you did to try to make it so.

'Cause something is happening and you don't know what it is Do you, Mr. Jones?

A thin man gets thin for lack. He sings to fill himself back up, and it takes many verses, some of them nonsense, like children's rhymes for babies who won't be soothed by reason or by rocking.

You babies. You big, dumb, beautiful babies.

Searching for Lila Moore: When a Friend Becomes Tangled Up in Blue

No one I know from college knows what happened to Lila Moore. This is something we all hate because Lila was probably one of the best, strangest, most darling people I've ever known, and she was one of my best friends in college. She was the best friend of a lot of people in college. How is it that not one of us knows if she's ok?

Because there's always the possibility that she's not. Upon first meeting, Lila gave one the impression of a quivering rabbit: soft, adorable, bright-eyed, heart beating like a trip hammer. Her father had been killed in an accident while she was in high school, which meant she had life insurance money and a deeply painful psychic scar. She wore a pair of diamond stud earrings and the same dingy pink tee shirt for days. One day, I looked at her and said, "Lila! Your hair looks so incredibly beautiful today," to which she replied, startled, "Thanks! I brushed it!"

There were periods in which "self-care" seemed as remote a possibility for Lila as her turning into an actual rabbit, even though my friend JE once witnessed her staring deeply into the eyes of one near the Administration building.

And there were other reasons to worry. Once, Lila was in the shower, while I was brushing my teeth.

"But you're not here anymore," I heard from the shower.

"What?" I said, turning to look. Two wide eyes peered out from the curtain's edge.

"Did I say something?"

"Out loud," I replied, unnerved by the look of fear that crossed my friend's face.

It was a look that indicated there was a conversation to which I was not privy but for which I would need to start listening, if I was to follow my friend into that fragile space her rabbit heart was making of her mind.

In the years that followed graduation, though, she seemed better, psychically happier, as she bounced from organic farm to organic farm. She was proud of her ability to do physical labor, to find her way through Mexico City on her own, to sleep alone on a beach—all actions that proved she was not "Baby Lila," as another friend called her, someone who needed taking care of. For a while, she returned to our college town and lived with a pair of friends, waitressing and taking pride, again, in the blue-collar labor, more akin to her father's life than to her own liberal arts college degree. While a waitress, Lila met Bill, a guy biking his way across the U.S., pulling a collapsible lawn mower behind him to make money on the way.

They married; I performed the ceremony, which included them standing in the broken bicycle rim that had forced Bill to stop in town, finding his way, magically, to the café where Lila worked. It seemed as if his misdirection re-directed her, delightfully, towards in no particular direction but happiness. She didn't need a man to save her . . . but at least, she wouldn't be alone with the voice inside.

If I've painted too much a picture of Lila as lost, an unstable, delicate creature, I have left out what made Lila magical. Lila knew ALL the words to ANY song, and the absence of her singing, in my life and in those lives of our friends, is what makes the radio silence of her absence an anxious one for me. It's not unusual, the loss of connection with a college friend, the end of the intimacy of late-night conversations, the sharing of developing selves, the connection faded because of distance or time.

But perhaps because Lila was never really, fully in the same place with us, fully in time with my friends, with me, we worry. And we miss her because the other place in which she seemed to reside was full of songs, so many lyrics, so many words crowding her inner life that surely a few had to escape as if in conversation with what we could not see. If one of us isn't there to hear her, how are we to know she is still able to sing in reply, isn't drowned out by the other voices in her head?

I went to see Lila and Bill once in North Carolina, and Lila confessed she was going to have a psychiatric evaluation, at the suggestion of her husband's psychiatrist father. I haven't heard from her since, but I hope— we all hope– she is still there, happily married and singing all the words to Bob Dylan's "Tangled Up in Blue," particularly. "Tangled Up in Blue" is the song of a journey between worlds, between lives. The protagonist falls in love with a woman *"married when [they] first met / soon to be divorced."* He sings that he "helped her out of a jam" but speculates that he "mighta used a little too much force." We learn how to love our friends as we learn to love ourselves in our youth, which means it is sometimes difficult to decide if you are being overly protective or if you aren't alarmed enough, when you should let go and when you need to intervene. In the song, the narrator leaves when things get messy: "she froze up inside," and he escapes, withdrawing because it is "the only thing [he] knew how to do."

I didn't withdraw, but I often wonder if Lila's "changed at all, if her hair is still red" because my past, like that of the protagonist in the song, is always close behind me. I always feel the need to check back in—but it's not because I don't feel like I took enough care of Lila. I think it's because, like the man in the song, *"all those people we used to know / they're an illusion to me now,"* and Lila's strangeness is still more beautiful to me, more loved than many of my stable, untroubled friendships of today.

Lila had access to a world that I loved to lean against, and I want to know if it still exists, if it is possible to exist half-magically in this world . . . or if you have to go crazy. Lila introduced me to the song and world of "Tangled Up in Blue": a world in which synchronicity, beauty, pain, absence, and hope co-exist and return, again and again. It is one of those songs I've loved so long that, if I didn't link it so closely to Lila, it would almost be too hard to find the origin of my love for it—almost as hard as finding the whereabouts now of Lila Moore.

Epilogue

A few years ago, we finally found her. If you're thinking "why didn't you all just use the internet?", you are young enough not to have experience with how a generation used to experience vanishing. A friend finally tracked down her mother's phone number just by using the online phone book, called her, then called Lila. Lila's fine: still married, teaching special education. She won Teacher of the Year. I called her once. When I asked her why she'd fallen out of touch, she said, "Oh, let's just not talk about that" and seemed embarrassed. We were worried, she said, for nothing. She said she wasn't really a phone call person, but she'd love it if I texted sometime. She says she's coming to my wedding. We all hope she is.

I Don't Enjoy the Silence

I'm at the Tractor Tavern's annual New Wave Cover Band Night: Love Vigilantes (the New Order band), For the Masses (Depeche Mode), and This Charming Band (Morrissey/The Smiths). It is epic. There is a light that will never go out, and people are people on a Blue Monday. I'm chatting up this charming man throughout the evening, and sometime during "Never Let Me Down Again," we began spontaneously choreographing little moves.

I miss Dena.

⌒〜〜〜⌒

My childhood town was so small that you spent most of your school years in class with the same 25 or 30 people. We all did kindergarten together, and then about a fourth of the class disappeared back out into the prairie to the two smaller elementary schools, where their dads could drop them off on their way to the grain elevators or where the buses could more easily run mud routes during thunderstorm season. The High Plains school was barely more than a shed, although the lunches were the envy of all the town kids; the mothers who lived nearby doubled as the school cooks and certainly never would have condescended to anything as lazy as store-bought bread. Dena went to the Catholic grade school, and I stayed in town.

But seventh grade marked the return of the country kids to the town school, and that's when I met Dena.

My mom says that, in kindergarten, she and Dena's mom watched us play together on the playground and that she had said, "I hope Dena and Bryn are friends. Dena seems brighter than the others." Dena's mother, Laura, was a thin, dark woman with the bright blue eyes and wide mouth possessed by all five of her children. Dena was the fifth and last: her oldest sister left for college the year Dena entered kindergarten. Dena's father was an old man; Laura was also old but eerily well preserved. Dena and I joked that her mother slept in ForeverWare, a reference to an episode of a television show we found hysterical, *Eerie, Indiana*, in which a mother put her twin sons in human-sized plastic containers to keep

15

them young forever. By the time Y2K came, Laura was deep into Apocalyptic Catholicism . Dena would write her master's thesis in sociology on the phenomenon.

But that was still to come. We were teens. We drove miles—the same mile over and over again—in my car, cruising first west to east, then north to south, and again. We walked everywhere one could possibly walk. Once, we walked through all of the alleys to de-familiarize ourselves with our town, long ago mastered. Once, we drove, slowly and carefully, in reverse through the entire town. We lay down in the middle of my street—the last street on the edge of town—and waited to see how long it would be before any car came by. Dena lived so deeply out in the country that she usually spent the whole evening after school at my house until midnight or one, when we would wake up my dad to jumpstart her pick-up, which always needed jumped. One Christmas, my dad wrapped up an old set of jumper cables and presented them to her, as a gift. We continued to wake him up.

We formed the one and only *Twin Peaks* club in town—indeed, we were the only ones who watched it. We each took on a character name from the show for the club meetings: Dena was Donna, and I was Audrey Horne. Donna, the best friend, though not of Audrey Horne—Audrey, forever with her unrequited crushes. We recruited a few additional members, crafting more and more elaborate induction rituals for each. For one full school day, Cynthia had to spin in circles whenever anyone said, "Lucy Lucy Lucy!" A few of our teachers caught on and would shout it at her as she passed down the halls. Together, we were benevolent ringleaders. Each year, in Spanish class, we produced a more and more ridiculous piñata to sell for the class fundraiser: one year, an iguana; the next, a rabid rat, with yellow teeth and strings of blood-red crepe paper hanging from them. We wrote haiku by the pound, mostly in biology class.

And music—music was always and everywhere. Music was a religion for Dena and me. We made each other tapes with obscure songs on them— I would hold the recorder near the television to capture bits of dialogue from Singles to put in between songs, and she would hold the recorder near the record player to capture Bobby Bare's "Skip a Rope," from a scratchy old record, belonging to her dad. It's true old country:

social critique, rather than the blindly patriotic schlock of today's country:

> *Stab 'em in the back / that's the name of the game*
> *And mama and daddy are the ones to blame*
> *Skip a rope / skip a rope / listen to the children while they play It's not*
> *really funny what the children say / skip a rope*

"You know?" one of us would say to the other, more of a statement than a question. "Yeah, I know," the other would reply, the agreement implied, the rationale unspoken. We weren't often quiet, but we felt we didn't always need the words.

But sometimes, we were quiet. We drove around silently, listening to OMD (Orchestral Maneuvers in the Dark, *Sugar Tax*), for instance, after Dena was crowned Homecoming Queen. It was much to her dismay. Our friend, the King, had had no choice but to follow the hetero-normative tradition defi ning so many small-town rituals, by which I mean he had to kiss her. It was her fi rst kiss, and, as we stood alone in the teachers' bathroom afterwards, the fi rst time I'd ever seen her cry. "Why couldn't they have just given me a certifi cate?" she angrily sobbed. "Why did they have to make us do that in front of everyone? Everyone says I seem really nice. But nobody really knows me." I would write my fi rst college essay about her: "Dena: The Human Geode." "Nobody" didn't mean me. I knew her. I knew how to get inside.

We cruised the one mile of our town for hours, listening to Erasure and making up elaborate synchronized arm movements we could both do, even while the other was driving. Secretly, we coordinated my Sundays to play piano for Mass with the Sundays on which Dena's family came into town for church, rather than attend their regular Marienthal service. I could collapse Dena in silent laughter with my choice of the post-homily instrumental music: say, the theme song from *Twin Peaks*. We went to see Depeche Mode, on the *Songs of Faith and Devotion* tour, the summer after our freshman year of college. We both agreed, virgins though we were, that if we had the chance, we would probably sleep with Dave Gahan, even though we'd probably get a disease. And, during "Never Let Me Down Again," when he sang the line "I'm taking a ride with my best friend," we pointed to each other.

Life really mattered to Dena and to me.

And then, in graduate school, she dumped me.

I didn't see it coming, of course—how else could it still hurt me as it does? Should I have seen it when we only visited each other at college two or three times, when we were only thirty minutes apart? Was it in the birthday cards and letters we still sent? The stories of new friends were caricatures for the other, certainly, but still, there'd be the friendly rat drawing we perfected on high school notebooks, the oldest joke that was never stale. Even our master's programs were near each other, although then, too, I visited her rarely, and she didn't have a car. Real friends didn't need constant connection, you know? We picked up where we left off, you know?

It seemed like we were still sharing: values, laughter, plans, futures. We both moved to the West Coast; we both entered PhD programs. And yes, she didn't always seem to see that as shared. I would ask her questions about her project; she would imply I couldn't really understand it. I referenced a critic who crossed disciplinary boundaries; she frowned and told me the literary use of that theory was inadequate. "You just study books," she said. "I study the world."

When Dena attended a conference in Seattle, of course, she stayed with me. But her irritation with me seeped into each eye roll, a slow drip onto the stone of her. On the last night, she told me that I was treating her like we were still in high school and that I had to know we weren't best friends anymore.

This is all I can tell you of this night—this and that I cried. Studies show that, in therapy, the closer a patient gets to the core of a trauma, the more fragmented their language becomes. I cannot remember more details, despite my unusually strong memory for them: I, who can remember what jacket you wore in kindergarten, the names of your first five kittens, although I could never remember the name of your dog. But I can remember that I thought it was unfair, still think that it was unfair—that she was unfair.

Even now, I want to say bitter things to fill in the blanks of that evening. I want to say I had always known we were different and never expected us to stay exactly the same, that if she felt like I had never changed how I treated her, it was because she never shared how she was changing. That if we were not friends anymore, it was not because of me. It was because of her.

Dena didn't stab me in the back, that's true. But it felt like she stabbed me squarely in the front, which is worse because I had to watch it happen. Later, she will send me an email apologizing for telling me in the way that she did, but still asserted I was treating her like we were in high school.

What could that possibly mean, I wondered? Treating her like life was important and funny and beautiful? As if we still had important things to say to one another that the other would value and understand? Why was that a hurtful thing?

For a while, she emailed me to tell me the big things: to explain why I wasn't invited to her wedding (they eloped), to tell me that she and her husband were moving to my state (the other side).

But I stopped feeling like I could really tell her anything anymore. You know? Do you? Because I don't. I don't know.

All I still ever need is one best friend, one person with whom to create and share a private world. But a best friend can be like uranium: an unstable but powerful element, with as much destructive capability as a lover and a half-life that will linger on well past its seeming disappearance. Of course, I am speaking of best friends who are no longer one's best friends. I have had other best friends more affectionate, more responsive, even, in the grander scope of things, more important. My remaining best friends are bound to me in compounds that change form without ever changing content, hydrogen and oxygen moving through our happy cycles indefinitely. But a best friend who is no longer . . . there is no sadness, no jagged hole like that created by such a loss. Time does not mitigate it, and Nostalgia cannot stitch it back together into a simple, non-reactive chain that remains unaffected by the violence done. It is unsurprising, then, confused as I still am, that I find myself mixing my metaphors, those last resorts. The tissue around the wound thickens, a raised map of injury that refuses to blend into my skin, a sensitive place that remains volatile, a half-life still active, although it seems as benevolently dormant as an empty nuclear factory.

This is becoming an old story. I write and rewrite it, thinking I will learn something new. The pages you just read were part of the first post I ever made on a blog I'd started, and I didn't think anyone read it, but Dena must have read it. We were at least in Facebook contact at that point, but after that post, she unfriended and blocked me. I guess I would say that it hurt her, but I wouldn't say I knew anything about Dena anymore by then.

When I began teaching creative non-fiction, we talked a lot about the stories you aren't ready to write. We'd listened to a *This American Life* piece on "Petty Tyrants," which, unsurprisingly, generated a lot of what is called "revenge prose" from students, as they wrote their own pieces. "Revenge prose" is when, no matter what the author says is the emotional core of the piece, the reader can tell that the *real* goal of the piece is to get back at someone, to make them look bad and their own selves look better. "If you feel like you're trying to defend something or prove something," I said, one day, "you're probably not ready to write it."

I said it because I'd been thinking about how to rewrite the Dena piece, how I hadn't been trying to get back at her, but how I had been trying both to defend myself and to prove something to myself. I'd been trying to defend myself from my own need for the conversation that never happened after she told us we weren't best friends anymore. She felt there was nothing more to say—she'd just wanted to say it and seemed ok continuing our friendship in a different form, although she would no longer be pointing at ME during "Never Let Me Down." So, I wrote a piece in lieu of that conversation. I didn't even ever think she'd read it. I still don't think it's mean—I still think what is clearest in that piece is that *I* still don't feel clear, that *I* still don't understand why we couldn't talk to each other anymore. But there I go—proving something again. Trying to prove that I tried to understand, to communicate, but the attempt was clumsy, incomplete, unchoreographed and out of sync.

Dena, I will try one more time to get out of my own way. Dena, this is the best that I can do:

I wasn't just startled you'd read the essay; I was startled you cared so much. I thought that if I could try to get distance from the break, and you'd initiated the break, that you already had the distance from a loss I couldn't seem to get. How little distance I had, I see now, and maybe my expectation that you wouldn't care reveals more about the distance that always permeated our friendship, like the air within molecules that seem bound together. Maybe we both were always distant from our own relationship, simply sharing ideas and jokes back and forth, without really listening for their impact on the other. In a way, we played our own version of "Skip a Rope"—playing at friendship but never hearing the lyrics, singing along as if we shared a melody instead of hearing the harmony of difference. So, when you finally spoke words to me that needed to have a separate meaning, I had so little practice hearing you as you, not us. I guess Depeche Mode was always right: *words like violence / break the silence / come crashing in / into our little world*. We crashed when the silence was deafening, and we finally, really had to speak to each other. Neither of us knew how to listen.

Pleasures remain / so does the pain. The pleasure of having such a creative, funny best friend remains, but I don't know now if I ever really knew you or if you really knew me. Artistically, I know the "therapist's couch" fi rst draft is raw with questions and with sadness: I was looking for someone to listen when the one who I thought always would was gone. Were you tired of listening to me and my emotions all the time? Were you finally starting to understand your own? Why did you think I wouldn't want to try and hear you? Now I know that "you know?" means so little— it's not knowing much. I wonder even now if my partner deludes himself, assuming I get him, and I know that love needs to be more than assumption of sameness. It is a song of faith and devotion: faith in growth, devotion to the mystery of molecules holding together.

I've read too many stories from my female students about losing their best friends, and none of them understand why either. "They were toxic," they want to tell me, to discard the pain like a worn-out high school tee shirt. But I tell them believing that is a form of self-harm. Your choice of a high school best friend is a gift you are trying to give yourself. You long for another to pull you into a more vibrant life, to give you access to bravery or joy or laughter, or you choose each other because you both share a difference, and difference is all that feels meaningful at 17. Dena, the first real cautionary lesson I learned in love was from you: that difference can't be shared forever. I wanted us to keep having reunion tours, but even at our peak, we were writing separate songs.

If I could tell you anything, Dena, it would be this: I wish you could know how much it hurt me not to understand you, but I accepted that the time for "you know?" is over. I wish I could tell you how glad I am, still, that we laughed and ran through alleys and did everything we could because we gave each other something closer to being our real selves, instead of being lonely. And I'm glad you found who you really are. I will always wonder if that person could have known me, as I really am, and loved me.

This charming man at the show is there with his own best friend, it turns out. "I can't tell you how much I love that guy," he shouts during "Enjoy the Silence."

You don't need to, I think. I know it: the wordless sense of belonging with your best friend, the way your very bodies would turn in unison towards the same lights and dance the same steps.

In a box, I have a weird medallion from the *Songs of Faith and Devotion* show—it's metal, with the astronaut from one of their videos on it. I keep it in that box with other broken things I don't seem to want to let go of. Maybe I'll give it to this charming man and keep trying to accept that, while I may not enjoy it, this story is always going to end in silence.

A Song with No Words for a Love that Could Not Speak Its Name or That of Any Other: A Fairytale of Sorts

Once upon a time, I would fall so passionately in love with a man that it could sometimes make me sick.

And once, even before that, this same man was walking through Volunteer Park, playing his bass. He was probably wearing a tank top, had probably smoked some weed, and was probably humming serenely. His eyes were sort of hooded and he had a small, myste-rious smile that made him look like George Harrison, my favorite Beatle. He, too, was a Quiet One.

The internet seemed to love the photo of my friend Jessica drinking our newest invention: The Whiskertini. Vodka, Chambord, sustainably harvested white whisker from my cat Judy as a garnish. Amid the "likes" and "ews," I saw his name. My heart warmed and stopped. Love is forever the fastest thermostat.

Turns out the Quiet One used to sell dessert with Jessica. And she didn't, at first, remember why or how they were friends. But I remembered every way I knew and felt him. The most important boyfriend of my 20s showed me what happens when you don't un-derstand how or why you love.

Anyway, this man heard drumming—good drumming—and he followed the sound, coming finally upon a curly-haired Muppet of a man with his full drum kit set up under one of the ginkgo trees. The two locked eyes, nodded, and jammed together for twenty min-
utes or more without speaking. They knew when to finish the song because they both felt when it was done. "I'm The Quiet One," said the man whose love would be a thick cord between my heart and his. "Hey, man," said the Muppet drummer. "I'm Jay."

This is how Jay and The Quiet One met, and this is how their band, Brothers, began. And this is how The Quiet One practiced.

The Quiet One didn't play music. He felt it. He intuited it from the ether. A friend told him about modern dance pioneer Martha Graham's phrase "blood memory," and he wrote a song about it, calling it, instead, "Blood Music." Like dancing, that song makes form fluid, runs deep into the spaces of the body that are beyond words. The Brothers were, after all, an instrumental trio, and they didn't need words—they ran deep enough on their own.

He was, to twist a phrase of Oscar Wilde's, the love that could not speak its name. "Could not"— so different than "dared not." While the love that dare not speak its name is closeted homosexual love— a love hindered by disapproval and the judgment of others- the love that cannot speak its name is what I had for this dark-eyed George Harrison; a love in which I was the only hindrance, my judgment clouded by my first full immersion in an emotion I couldn't articulate or handle.

I say "immersion" because loving him felt like drowning.

This wasn't his fault. The Quiet One was the most loving, the kindest, the hottest. There was so much love. I did understand that, before him, I had not known sexual passion, what it meant to really make love. He was good, in all ways.

It brought out the worst in me.

When I met the third member and asked him what he did, he stared at me and replied, scornfully, "You mean, for money? I'm a waiter," and I felt ashamed. The three of them would build songs together, listening, responding, finding their way through the music like blind men touching bolts of silk. When one of them would improvise for an extended period of time and really "get it," they would nod at each other, ask later, "You go to Havana, man?"

"Going to Havana"—that place beyond words. They put out two CDs, but they didn't really care who heard them. Once, I went to a gig and was the only audience member. They laughed and played and played, until they were all in Havana, and it didn't even matter where I was.

There's a famous modern dance piece called *Kiss* in which two dancers swing towards each other in harnesses. Whenever their ropes twist, the female dancer slowly, painfully pulls away, spinning away from the body against which she was, a moment ago, so blissfully pressed. After the first year, as our differences became more notable than the chemistry, I felt like that every day—involved in an untangling, rather than a simple break-up. I fell in love with the Mark Twain American (see "Paint It Blacker"). I fell in love with the Painter (see "Sound and Vision.") Every day, I would walk the Burke-Gilman trail to school and catalogue the lies I was telling to cover my affairs, those weak attempts my spirit made to show my weaker flesh this was not the man for me. *I am not a liar. I am a truthful person*, I'd tell my bewildered self each day. Each day, I'd hear my rational self struggle up, as if through dark water, gasping: *Then why are you doing this?*

I didn't know. That is, I couldn't talk about this love in ways that made me feel at home with my heart. I knew it was love. But drowning . . . it did also feel like drowning. I'm a Libra, a sign of the air. I'm at my best in mental free play with someone's mind. I used to wonder, in my twenties, if I even really had a body. The Quiet One was a Taurus. Earth. The Bull. All body, all earth. As we fell in love, I physically felt a cord between the two of us, like the one from which the dancer struggled to unwrap her own separate cord. That cord was real, and heavy. Like a lung, fi lling up slowly, with anything but air.

That was the problem with The Quiet One: I couldn't always tell if it mattered, if I really mattered, because, at first, he wouldn't tell me how he felt. He lived upstairs from me and took to hanging out on the porch when he knew that I'd be home. I could tell he liked me, and I was ambivalent. "He never really talks, and I hate his goatee," I'd tell my roommate Gretch-en, wrinkling my nose. I thought I'd give him a chance, though, and so, I did what I do with all quiet people: I asked him questions. What was your favorite birthday party? When was the last time you were really afraid? How do you feel about your mother? And The Quiet One resisted—or that's how it felt. "Aw, man, that stuff will just come out," he'd say, stretching his limbs out across the couch we kept on the porch. "Let's just hang out."
Let's just be in Havana.

But that was not how I hung out. I was a high-wire act, rushing out into adventure and vulnerability, with nothing underneath me, no net, even less of a sense of how far down I might fall. I was a graduate student who made her living analyzing other people's dialogues. Words, for me, were at the crux of all intimacy. I didn't fall in love—I talked myself into it. I talked myself out of it. I found out what I felt not by feeling it but by processing it out loud. I read Leslie Jamison's essay "In Defense of the Sacchrin(e)" and heard myself in her own words: "This is how writers fall in love. They feel complicated together, and then they talk about it." I wanted a 1000-word essay from each lover on why my eyes should open on him every morning. How could I sit on this couch in silence? What could I feel with that?

A lot, it turns out. While I never stopped needing words, The Quiet One was persistent, patient, and we fell. He'd George Harrison smile at me, reach for me, and down, down we'd go, an aerial trick with no net, exquisite in its freefall.

Our love was visceral, not verbal, and that was a problem for me. Even in our music, that silence was present. Though we both considered ourselves "hippies," the word meant different things. I was the hippie of folk music: the Indigo Girls, Bob Dylan, and blue grass; he favored world

music and tablas or Jaco Pastorius, World's Greatest Bass Player. That first
summer, we would ride around in his jeep listening to Akbar Ali Khan,
and he would look at me all the things that could ever be said. He sang
little made-up songs about me constantly, which I loved. Our favorite was
"Come and Stay, My Love." It went something like this: "Come and stay,
my love / You'll never have to leave, my love." We hummed it often. Once,
dreamily listening to John Coltrane, I was startled out of my reverie by the
realization that something was familiar. "Wait! This is 'Come and Stay, My
Love'!" It had been subliminally remixed in his mind, those chords so deeply
played inside of him that they were not longer recognizable as anything but
his own heart. That stuff comes out, unintentional plagiarism. When you
believe something is your own, but it is not.

*There was one word, though, The Quiet One used often with me. That word was
"No." I'd suggest that we go out for drinks. "No," he'd say, "let's watch a movie." I'd
ask if he wanted to take a walk. No, it was cold—and he had that new song to practice.
Brunch before the Market? No, and then he'd be hungry at 3:00, that witching hour
when all restaurants have stopped serving lunch and haven't yet started serving dinner.
Once, angry at him, I accused him of being Balkan. "You ALWAYS say no first when
I suggest something, even if you want to do it! It's like it has to be your idea, or you don't
want to do it. Why do you balk? Are you from the Balkan States?" He laughed at
that, and then said, "No."*
    *I see it now—that he said no because he struggled with words,
couldn't easily express so much of what he wished to say, that, like me,
he was in love and frightened by the depth of the feeling, afraid, as I was, that we didn't
"get" each other. He said no so he could pause, regain some sense of control, some way to
find a place in this thing that rushed, like the ground, up to meet the falling. But to the
Me of that time, it felt like rejec-tion, and it felt like I was being shut out.*

My favorite song in high school was Depeche Mode's "Enjoy the
Silence." Why was it, exactly, that I couldn't enjoy it with him? Twenty years
later, I can see the value in merely "liking" something for its own sake,
the appreciative "like" of a photo with a Whiskertini, but I couldn't then.
I needed to understand everything, to know why my heart felt like it did,
how that cord could hold me to someone without choking me, how, as in
James Baldwin's "Sonny's Blues," deep water didn't have to mean drowning.
But understanding is not the same thing as acceptance. Love itself will not
always throw you a rope.

When I cheated on him with the Mark Twain American[1], it was, of course, because of words. The MTA was a poet, and he had so many words, so very many words and so many ways to say yes. I couldn't say no.

So I didn't.

That first summer, when we still lived a floor apart, was the hardest—in love but not at peace. I would watch him silently as he slept. I didn't, couldn't sleep for months. One night, in the dark, I put on Duke Ellington's "Fleurette Africaine" and tried to let it be enough to fill the silence I felt between me and this beautiful man, tried to trust in the beauty of a song without words, as I would until the end. I had nowhere to go but down, where it would have also been impossible to sleep, knowing he was above.

The Quiet One and I broke up, would break up five more times over the course of two and a half years. I moved to another house after the first year, he moved three times; each space was a new chance to find a way together by living apart. Each space also was just that: more space—space apart, space where I could fall in love with other men. But we made it past that first break-up into a much, much better phase of our relationship. How we did it taught me almost all of the words I now need to understand love: I love you, I'm sorry, I need this, I am hurt. I learned that silence didn't have to mean it was over, and he became more open, more able to talk about his fears and hopes for us. Once he came home from band practice, giddy with the pleasure of self-awareness: "Brynny! Guess what? We were trying to decide what to work on, and Jay wanted to start a new song, but I said, no, we should keep practicing the old one, and he said, 'Man, why do you always have to say no first?' I am a Balkan!"

We were never on the same page, but that was because I needed a page, a place onto which we could write our story. And The Quiet One was a musi-cian, his page lined with staffs and black notes. But I did learn how to feel. Really feel.

We lived together for one month, just before our second-to-last break-up, but when he moved out, The Quiet One left me a list of all the things he loved most about me, all the precious things we'd given each other during our years together. One of them was this: "Thank you for leading me out of the Balkan States." So many words, in the end. It brings tears to my eyes even now, as I write this, and sometimes, still, I am so sad thinking of him, wishing I could have sat quietly next to him in the air, humming along to those songs without words.

But my own heart needed what it did, and my body needed sleep and peace. I pushed one final time away, and two bodies twisted in the space, alone but one no longer drowning.

---

1   See "Paint it Blacker"

27

Emily walks in, bearing a homemade bouquet of beet roses. Each beet is carved into petals, and they drip beautifully down to the greens. As usual, I am impressed by her handiness. "Emily, those are amazing." As usual, she cocks an eyebrow, murmurs "Thanks," and skitters away. I turn to Cara. "Why doesn't she like me? This is the fifth time I've met her, and she acts like I'm going to eat her." Cara looks sideways at Emily, now presenting the birthday girl with the bouquet. "Emily is like all of us—she needs to know where to stand in the room to avoid being hit."

"All of us" meant the Pine Street girls. They were my ex-boyfriend's best girlfriends, a tight circle of intelligent, emotional, dangerous women. If damage breeds more damage, abuse more abuse, this friend group was like a pedigreed racehorse's family tree, each member a purebred of unhappiness and post-traumatic stress. Not one of them had escaped physical abuse at the hand of a parent, hadn't picked up their drunken mother's bottles or excused their angry father's tirade.

And then there was me. Whenever I complained about grad school or eagerly anticipated my own mother's visit, worrying about whether she would enjoy the arboretum more than a trip to Vancouver, I could see the hashtag "#youhaditeasy" float in vapor, unspoken but there.

But I didn't see the anger coming because some of them warmed to me immediately, like Cara. Cara was the Quiet One's best friend and the only person I now wish I'd never met, about whom I have actually said, "She did a number on me." I ascribe a severe spiral into depression in my late 20's to Cara's unique ability to convince me that even the most benign of my actions was a secret attempt to wound her deeply, that when I saw myself, I could not see myself for the thoughtless beast I really was. And I could not break away from her spell. In fact, I was more attracted, initially, to Cara than to my boyfriend. She was dry and excitable at the same time, and she could laugh without opening her mouth, which made it look like she was choking on milk, like laughing was painful.

She was, it is fair to say, brilliant, majoring in the Comparative History of Ideas, her senior project on the management of her own death. She researched all aspects of it: who would touch her body, what legal rights a friend or a parent would have to determine her final handling. She assigned particular friends the duties best suited to them as a means of controlling her own anxiety about death. The Quiet One, kind and patient, got Care of the Spirit: if she was violently murdered, we were to talk to him, and he would counsel us away from rage, ask us to consider "what Cara would want."

The longer I knew her, the more I began to fathom what an impossible task that might be: to know what Cara would want. Staring into you, holding your hand, Cara would tell you she adored you, explaining that it was precisely because she loved you that she had to tell you that you were, in fact, a monster, your actions unforgivable, unbelievable, unlovable. The scale of the action was not important—what was important, she always said, was that you should have known how it would hurt her. Under her gaze, unwavering, you wondered how long you had lived like this, an archer of injury, how you had managed to get away for so long with your careless, heedless actions, with your silly, naïve life.

Borderline personality disorder is marked, traditionally, by what's simply called "emotional instability"; one with BPD experiences others in terms of idealization and devaluation, their perception of you fluctuating rapidly between the two. One of the most famous books on the disorder is called, suitably, *I Hate You—Don't Leave Me*. It is a condition difficult to define and diagnose, according to the DSM, because it implies there is a flaw in one's personality, instead of in one's psyche or brain. Everyone has preferences, triggers—do these always have to be pathologized?

According to Cara, the first time I betrayed her was with a guy who only read magazines. The Magazine Guy had gone on two dates with Cara, before they both stopped suggesting they meet up again. He and I had met on their second date—a dinner party for another Pine Girl. He knew I was dating The Quiet One, so when we ran into each other on campus one day, and he suggested we get a drink, I thought it seemed innocent enough. Still enthralled with Cara, I was also curious: what could possibly be unattractive to a man about Cara?

"I mean, isn't she just so VAST?" I gushed over a gin and tonic. "She's so insightful, so intelligent, so . . .world-full." He looked at me and lowered his drink. "Yes . . . I just feel like with Cara, that vastness could so easily be a vale of tears."

Cara was not a vale. Cara was an ocean. One minute, she glittered on the surface; the next, she was the storm, the spirit of Calypso, angry that you dared traverse her waters. I would apologize to Cara for having drinks with The Magazine Guy, and, over the next three years, for asking her to have dinner with my mom and me, for telling her I had feelings for another man who was not The Quiet One, for coming into the house without knocking when I'd been doing so for a year, for staying overnight with The Quiet One when I *should have known* she was not happy with me that day.

I do—and did—see how so many of these things might have seemed, in fact, potentially hurtful. Even dinner with my mom would mean, for her, watching my mom and I interact with kindness, trust, love—all those things her own mother withheld from her. The Quiet One was her best friend, so even if I reached out to her as my friend, telling her I'd fallen in love with someone else put her in an awkward spot. But it was the rise and the fall, the unpredictability as to when something was no big deal versus a revelation of your active and monstrous manipulations intended to hurt that came to frighten me, over time. I began to doubt myself, found myself wondering why no one else but Cara noticed how terrible I was, under this shiny veneer of being a good person.

It is also true that therapists are often uncomfortable labeling women with Borderline Personality Disorder because often, feelings of abandonment or physical abuse are at the root of a fierce internal competition to see others as allies or enemies, those whom you love easily becoming those you should fear. With family problems that are never another's to tell, Cara might more justly be diagnosed with Post-Traumatic Stress Disorder, an arrow wound in the target of her own body.

It was Cara who introduced me to the Joni Mitchell song, "All I Want," a song that would permanently link troubled loves with pure desires for me. She once misheard the lyrics *wanna knit you a sweater / wanna write you a love letter* as *wanna knit you a letter / wanna write you a love sweater.* She immediately went to work knitting a letter to a new man, one who couldn't yet suspect even a sweet gesture like this was potentially a knitted letter bomb.

In memory now, I think back to the last time I saw her, in a red-walled bar, in the middle of winter. It is my favorite bar, and I am looking forward to seeing Cara, glad that we can still be friends after my break-up and reunion with the Quiet One. For Cara, it is a return to battle under the auspice of love.

I say how glad I am that we are friends again, and how even though I knew she didn't like us dating again, that we would all recover, over time. Her eyes narrow: like the Kraken, I arise, suddenly a monster. Her face goes cold and angry, a sight so familiar that I instinctively recalibrate, scrolling quickly back to see what word, exactly, I said to initiate the change. As usual, I come up with a blank, and as she furiously puts on her mittens, I grab her wrists and attempt to calm her down. "Cara, wait, stop, what happened?" "You KNEW I was uncomfortable with you coming over again . . . and . . .and you did it ANYWAY," she hisses, extricating herself from my pleading hands. She walks out the door, and I stare at our two glasses of port before the long exhale tells me something I didn't know I'd want to feel: I am relieved. I hear myself say "Whoa" out loud. I realize I am also glad.

She's gone, and I realize if I just let her go, don't run after her or come to her on my knees later, I no longer have to worry about where to stand in the room. If she is right about me, then I deserve this punishment, but I don't yet understand the pattern of offenses. The punishment is, for now, merely confusing. I will need leave this room and find a space where the borders don't shift like quicksand—a place where my identity always matches my passport without questions or suspicion of forgery. I will need other experiences to see if I am horrible, other people's eyes and testimonies. If she is not right, if I am not thoughtlessly cruel, then I am lucky she keeps on walking.

I am in the Corcoran in Washington, D. C. Everywhere, I am surrounded by the Annie Leibovitz exhibition, *A Photographer's Life,* and everywhere, I am undone by the evidence of love.   There are, of course, the
famous *Rolling Stone* images, the ones loved by the world: giant prints of
naked John Lennon and clothed Yoko Ono, Meg and Jack White as
circus performers with Meg strapped to a wheel and Jack aiming a dag-
ger. But this exhibition also contains the photos of a dead Susan Sontag:
of Annie taking care of Sontag, of Sontag being wheeled onto planes to
the Fred Hutchinson Cancer Center in Seattle, and, finally, controver-
sially, of her corpse, alone.   I look at that thin, still body, the signature
shock of white hair, and I know that all of these images are love.

But I am newly in love, and death is far off in the background
of my world. I'm still in Act One, and Mortality is merely a dusty prop
in a dark corner, to be exposed once, only, in the very final scene, the
very last act. I know that I see love, but my love has never died---will
never die, I think. And so, I have to round the corner before I find the
photograph that undoes me and brings tears of recognition.

Small, square-framed amidst two or three other minor works, it
is a picture of a handful of seashells. "Susan's Shells," it's called. I weep
openly. Strangers look over to see if they are missing another picture
of the corpse, squint at the tiny image, glance sideways at me. After all
the chemo and bones and death and pain, Annie Leibovitz took pictures
of her lover's things. She took pictures of the shells because Susan was
loved, and because Susan loved them, the shells are loved. The shells
are love. . I am surrounded even here by love: these images of what the
lover has left, in the end. The beloved, the beloved may be dead, but
still her objects remain, and anything she touched with her notice has
become love: all that it was and all that remains. I am surrounded by
love. And because I am in love, I feel this, and I weep.

I go back to Alexandria, Virginia, to my beloved's home to which I
have a key, and I feel it again.   I am here again from Missouri, and I
let myself in with this key his hands have touched. I feel it again in his
closet. Sam's shirts. Surrounded by these artifacts of him, imbued with
their "him-ness," the smell of him, I am surrounded by this love of him
concretely: tactile, viscous, the densest reality of this man with whom I
am in love, perhaps more than I've ever been. I sigh with happiness to

be this close to him, even amidst the merest traces. He seems so present that I turn, instinctively, to look for him in the doorway. But he is on a business trip, and I am here in his closet, looking through his stuff for evidence, the proof that his divorce was the best thing ever to happen to him and to me.

♱

I am a snoop. If you are in a relationship with me, and I have not yet sounded out the depths of your heart, unpacked and analyzed the degree to which you love me, I will secretly read your diary, pour over your photo albums, maybe look under your bed to find, among the dust bunnies and crumpled, mislaid receipts, the measure of your love for me. It is not that I am empty, low on self-esteem and skittish in my trust, but rather that I cannot accept "enough" when I could find out "more." I am a museum with a permanent source of funding; I am the curator herself, rubbing her hands with glee over each new acquisition, considering its possibilities, reconstructing the exhibit again and again. I know each love is a story with the details missing, with multiple threads, and the fuller I can make the story, the more of it I can tell. And feel. And tell again.

This is the story, the story of Sam and Bryn. It is one of infinite possibilities and which bears infinite retellings—a strong initial framework, rife with blank spaces, waiting to be filled with evidence that once you find your real love and you lose them, they will always come back:

We meet in Kansas, 1994, both in separate graduate programs, but he walks into the used bookstore where I work, and he smiles at me. I think to myself—I really do: "He is the handsomest man I have ever seen." He approaches the desk.

"Hey, do you have a copy of The History of Saturday Night Live?"

In my head: "Oh god, and he is funny, so lovely, the man of my dreams."

Not in my head, out loud: "No, but if you leave your name and phone number, I can call you if it ever comes in."

The book comes in the very next day.

We become friends of a sort, despite his girlfriend, on whom I ask him to cheat before he returns to New York; he will say thank you and gently refuse, in the third email I ever receive. I will receive one email from him every year, and so, we stay in touch.

And when he visits me in Seattle, 2003, just before they get en-gaged, I am mid-way through my doctorate and my own happy relation-ship. It will not seem so strange, although I have my suspicions, suspi-cions confirmed years later, in bed, when I ask him why he visited then, why I was not invited to the wedding. Sam turns to me and holds my face. "She wanted to get married, but I couldn't sleep. I couldn't sleep, so I came to see you. And you seemed so happy. I wanted to invite you, but you were the hope, and I couldn't bear to see you."

We are that story: old friends with bad timing. It bears retelling.

We decide to retell it. I am a professor in Missouri when she leaves him in 2007, and the email I receive is, somehow, not entirely surprising: "I'm getting divorced and will be in Kansas in May. Want to meet up?"

It is not surprising—is this not how the story goes?
We meet again in Lawrence, Kansas—not the city of our meet-ing but the city in between that of the business trip bringing him back to Kansas, and the small, depressing university town to which I've willingly exiled myself, not fully anticipating the loneliness of the single, small-town professor. We decide to meet at his hotel room. Between us, we have eleven years of unconsummated desire, an implicit agreement that we are soul mates, permission newly granted. And we meet at a hotel room.

Is this not how the story goes?

We begin to fly back and forth between Missouri and Washing-ton, D. C. I take to singing the Magnetic Fields' song "Washington, D. C.," joyful in its specificity, how it's about him, it's about me:

> *Washington, D. C.*
> *it's paradise to me*
> *It's not the people doing something real*
> *it's not the way that springtime makes you feel no no no It ain't no*
> *famous name on a golden plaque*
> *That keeps me that makes me ride that railroad track It's my*
> *baby's kiss that keeps me coming back*

Occasionally, he has more business trips—one or two days during the three or four I visit. I stay, rather than return to my miserable town, consider these days in D. C. without him my chance to try out being the second wife. I prowl the rooms, feel out a space for myself in this home recently abandoned by the first one, familiarizing myself with his neighborhood, his life, his things.

By which I mean I snoop.

⌁

Still in the closet. The mother lode is behind the shirts. I push aside a box of files and find a giant document, beautifully illuminated with scrollwork, elaborately framed. It's the first ketubah I've ever seen, but I recognize it from the mini-lessons in Judaism Sam's been giving me —an explanation of a blessing here, *"you cover the bread so it doesn't get embarrassed,"* a definition of a word there, a *"lulav"* is a palm frond. I gather in the lessons greedily: Sam's faith. I laugh when others ask if he is trying to convert me. "No," I say. *"Not yet,"* a part of me whispers, hearing the echoes of the not-yet-ex-wife, the phrase "cultural differences." But here it is, this ketubah, her explicit agreement that even if she is not Jewish, their children will be . . .and that she will love him forever, as will he. I find his signature (*Sam's signature*) and read the lines: "And I, Samuel Edward, say to my beloved, Sara Renee . . . ."

It is beautiful. But I am the beloved now. It moves and irritates me, these words of forever dismissed after two years of marriage. Our story is just as long as theirs, and our marriage will be longer. Is that not how the story goes?

I set the heavy frame aside, impatient, glimpsing the wedding album stacked in the corner. This object better fits my need for evidence, contributing to the details of my collection in a more satisfactory way. Images never lie like words. These photographs are sepia-toned, as if from an event well in the past, one for books closed, books of mistakes not likely to be repeated. There are many posed family portraits and few candids, and the curator inside likes this: the "not us" portion of our love's retrospective. I will give it not even a full wall, this marriage never meant to be, a function of convention, John Lennon and Cynthia, Jack and Meg White's brief marriage before the real fame came, the youthful, unquestioned "next step," later justly questioned.

The curator ignores the fact that it is the wife, the first one, who did the questioning. Beloved, beloved . . . the writing actually on their wall. "I, the beloved, promise to break these solemn vows, beloved, once loved, I will no longer love." Even as I look through this album, this bride's face looks happily out at mine, and I know she is beginning life again with another, the bad one; they are the cheaters. I know this from her blog. My search is not limited to this home. An academic knows to diversify her sources. A curator will accept an anonymous donation, if it serves her purposes.

I close the album, full of his pain, giddy with the pleasure that I know it now. It's not enough, and I want more. And then I know it's here, somewhere. If all these things were kept, there is another object in this house. I will trace the failure of this marriage to its first object. I will find it and know it all. Love him fully. And somehow, I will know that I am, too. Loved more than her.

I look for some place small. Like me, my lover believes in ritual, and so, I think like him. That's how it is, in these stories: two hearts, one mind.

And I find it sooner than you'd think: in the small, shallow drawer of his valet.

His wedding ring is placed inside another circle—a bracelet of beads, protecting it from further harm. It is a gesture so Sam, I catch my breath. *Sam's gestures.* I pick it up, note the two diamonds inside the band, and (*I do*), I put it on.

It is, predictably, too big for me, but there's a coldness to this ring. I feel less, not more. I feel, in fact, so small: smaller than this world I've made of Him and Me, smaller than a shell.

Even if this ring did fit, I know with sudden clarity what fact this evidence supports. I am not inside this circle. In fact, I am so far out of it that it embarrasses me. I need to be covered, like bread. This is the truth. It's not the truth I meant to find. It is, however, the truth that must be faced, and for now, there is no other corner to turn and find my face in love.

This is what it means to go through a divorce. You exit a life that has been years in the making, and you leave it so fast, you leave a wake—not breadcrumbs leading you back to home but the pieces of the home itself. They've led me to see that you are the one who never wanted to leave, the one who can't yet break the circle. I have presumed that I could break it, reform it in my own image, simply by looking to understand you, my love, my darling, by feeling out these crumbs of a home and thinking they were mine. But they are not mine, just as no collection of you can ever make you mine.

This is the end of this story. Beloved, beloved—there is a blank space in another story not my own, a story of you, a stranger, this quiet hoarder. Here is all the proof you'll ever need that, once, you were not loved enough, not even enough for her to take the wedding china or these photos and save you from the things that were your things together. I know now these things will never be my things. This is not my story. I will not be the next wife.

Practice Room: Elliott and the Bands He Couldn't
(Wouldn't) Quit

It's two weeks after Elliott and I start dating, and I am at Northwest Folklife, the Memorial Day weekend local arts festival, watching a 60-something-year-old drum majorette twirl her baton, hilariously, while sitting down. He is a few rows behind her, the only trumpet player under 60. It's a good gag: the Ballard Sedentary Sousa Marching Band.

I go to all their shows.

I also go to many of the shows of Elliott's other band, the one we call his "Bro Band" because it is full of guys he would never hang out with—nice enough but married and living in suburbs so far away that it takes one of them an hour to get to practice. They play covers of radio hits we don't listen to. The summer I am in England, co-leading a study abroad trip, they tease him about possibly having killed me. "Oh, Bryn's 'still in Europe'? Yeah, right, Elliott—you're the last one they'd suspect." He likes it when they tease him—it makes him feel like he belongs.

Elliott often doesn't belong—in either band. He comes home from Bro Band one night, humiliated. "I tried to make a joke about something, and it failed, miserably." He wouldn't tell me about what. He hates that they are learning a Maroon Five song; his favorite song is "We Sing in Time" by the Lonely Forest. He gets tired of playing Sousa at the Leif Erikson Hall or the Ballard Locks and complains about losing Saturdays to their gigs. "Why do you stay in?" I ask, as we walk to the car with his trumpet, waving goodbye to those who notice we're leaving. "Oh, it's kind of nice to keep my chops up. It can be fun." He IS adorable in the old-school band uniform they give him to wear. He stays in the Bro Band because the lead singer is a friend of a friend.

I don't mind being a band girlfriend, though I am considered the performer of the couple. I'm the one who breaks the ice, who sings first at karaoke, who tells the stories of our lives at parties as if we're around a campfire. Our friends all call us "Bryn and Elliott"—not "Elliott and Bryn." But I don't need to be the star. I like watching him enjoy himself, know how much he loves playing trumpet, no matter his lukewarm commitment to either band.

But Elliott thinks I mind. He thinks I mind it when he leaves to go practice. Here's the thing: that's not what I mind. I mind that we have been together for years, and he still sees his apartment, where he never sleeps, which seems to have become a very expensive underpants storage unit, as the place where he gets to do the things he likes. I mind that when I ask him what scares him most when we talk about getting married or moving in together, he can't come up with an answer. I mind that when I ask him why he stays with me, then, he doesn't seem to think being in love and having fun are good answers. He still feels like he's losing himself, that I am the lead singer, and he struggles to be heard.

But most of all, I mind that I see myself becoming yet another girlfriend in his relationship pattern. Our couples therapist will say near the end, "Elliott doesn't say 'no,' but he relies on you hearing 'maybe.'" He stays with his high school girlfriend (just a friend who pushed for more) until late in college, when he begins what will be an eleven-year relationship with another woman (just a friendship that became more). He stays and stays, even when he was always uncertain of the former; even when he's stopped loving the latter, he stays for two more years. And now there's me. *But I am different,* I think. *He fell in love with me from the start.* I'd always thought I was like Penny Lane from Cameron Crowe's *Almost Famous*—the lovable groupie who gets to ride the tour bus because she loves the music. She also thinks she's special. I realize now thinking you're special is its own kind of dangerous thinking: not like a groupie but like a star. If you're never surprised by groupies at the door, it takes you longer to see the limitations of adoration when one person does not feel equal. You always assume they'll stay, not go.

When finally I hand him the paper bag with the remaining items left at my house (a hand-blender, a shirt, a small fox I'd given him, some sheet music), I will ask him why he doesn't want our life, one more time, again. "I always felt there was a tension," he says, averting his eyes. I hear: "I never felt like I belonged."

He has his Saturdays back now, and the late nights to work on editing photos—another activity from which he felt I kept him. It was a habit he'd developed when he wasn't in love with the long-term girlfriend—working late into the night on projects, instead of going to bed with her. I imagine I see him now: he works and works, now eleven o'clock, now midnight, never in the bed but never leaving the bedroom. His trumpet case sits on the floor with the music he needs to learn but doesn't really like. He knows he will practice it, though. You have to know your part if you want to belong.

Jingle Bells: An Elegy

It starts because we both think my unpredictability has become predict-able. Elliott finds it hilarious. I look up in the middle of reading to do it, stop stirring risotto or petting the cat and turn to him. "Hey," I say, "Name that tune." Without breaking eye contact, I begin to tap on his arm. Dat dat daaaa dat dat daaaa da dat da da daaa. "Jingle bells!" he says, breaking into a smile.

It is always "Jingle Bells."

It becomes one of our favorite things about each other: this game that pretends to offer surprise, that requires close attention to the message being tapped, like Morse code, onto the other's body. But really, we know it is a ritual communicating certainty, a sly wink to the other in the face of the unknown. *I know where this is going, but I will pretend I don't,* his eyes smile at mine. *And when it goes there, we will have gone there together.*

I decide it will be our first dance at our wedding.

I imagine his delight as I announce, in a beautiful, creamy dress, a glass of champagne in my hand, that I have chosen a very special song for this first dance, and the song begins—Frank Sinatra's version, or may-be that of Sammy Davis, Jr. He laughs as I prance towards him, and we join hands. We swirl in a big circle, enclosed inside arms and an inside joke.

But there is no wedding because I've been playing the wrong game. And that's not what this ever was, I thought, it's not what love is—there should be no games, I know. Except it seems there are, and it is a game in and of itself to pretend there aren't.

There are games of strategy, which I attempted to avoid, the clearer it became he really didn't want to get married. These games you didn't even know you played, and yet, you find yourself browsing through articles with titles like "How to Get Him to Move in with You" or "How to Tell If He's Never Going to Be Ready."

There are the weeks you spend together, structured with points and pathways like a board game: pick up your piece and go to the farm-ers' market; buy a half-flat of raspberries for half-price (bonus points). Proceed to Monday, Tuesday, your weekly viewing of "How I Met Your Mother" (watched late because of band practice). Thursday—Standing Date with Friends (overdid the drinking again! Lose one turn and some of his respect).

There are games of chance ("We're at the Pac Inn—join us for a drink, if you're on your way home!") and team challenges ("do we invite them or not?") and individual foot races ("don't kiss me now—I have a cold"). There are mind games, but these mostly feel benevolent, recast as "relationship discussions," in which I sit on the couch beside you, the cat sleeping behind our heads, and love you as you try to come up with something, anything, to explain why you do not want this life you've built with me. I draw a reverse play card, turn this game upon myself: this is not about me, this love is worth more than your pride, Bryn, not everyone is as quick with words as you are.

There are rules of engagement, but the engagement never happens. He tells me that at some point, he felt like we stopped being on the same team. I look back at our life for the evidence of this: the way he'd anticipate I would want the fl our back on my side of the counter as we cook, my careful scanning of menus, during Restaurant Week, for anything that could kill him, the sand squirrel he made me on Ruby Beach, the book I bought him this last Christmas about how to draw a chicken. Even when I think of the anguished couch discussions, I think of holding his hand, think, *This is what love is.*

There were different teams? When had the game changed? What was so hard about the higher levels, when marriage, maybe a baby, seemed only like extensions of the game we were playing together, the one I called *We're So Lucky?*

Draw six cards, return to go. No roll of dice to make our relationship move forward, but the movements I miss now are these: the whirling in the kitchen, as I grabbed him for "Surprise Dance," the intuitive rearrangement of limbs as one person turns on their side in sleep, the tapping of my fi ngers to a tune that will not be guessed, a tune tapped, now, on air.

Despite my love of Stevie Nicks's clothes, I was never into Fleetwood Mac before The Barback, who converted me to at least really appreci-ating "Big Love." The Barback could belt it out like nobody's business, but the Lindsay Buckingham guitar part is, by The Barback's own admis-sion, a bitch. Fast, hard, and ever-changing in its rhythmic emphasis, the guitar murmurs intensely, a schizophrenic muttering on the bus, before it bursts, an intricate attack, and the chorus promises to leave your Stevie Nicks ass in search of REAL love. Big Love.

When The Barback first saw Buckingham play that song live, he thought, "I'll never be able to play that song."

When The Barback first met me, he was 19, and I was his 29-year-old grad assistant professor. When he and I fell in love, 11 years later, he was (again, by his own admission) a wreck—a single father with a chronic illness, a smoker of many things, living at home, and still suffering, clearly, from the PTSD of his last, unhappy relationship with a narcissistic make-up artist. But we both (foolishly) thought, "Why can't we be in love? We'll just take it day by day."

"But then I thought: Why can't I learn how to play that song?" The Barback told me, as he sat strumming it on my couch. "If I at least start practicing it, a little bit every day, I've got to be able to do it at some point, right?" I loved him on that couch. I loved him everywhere.

We tried to date, despite the fact that he worked from 9 p.m. until 4 a.m. and I worked among the living. I tried hard to accept that his smoking and his preference for Red Bull to real food were not deal-breakers. He tried to believe me when I said I believed in him.

After practicing the song for over year, The Barback could still only play about halfway through. He could play it really well, really beau-tifully, but at some point, he'd have to stop, shaking out his cramping hand. "My arm gets tired," he'd say to me, sheepishly putting down the guitar. "I just don't have the strength."

We fell in love so hard. "I can't stop thinking about you as my wife," he said one night at a party, pulling me aside and holding my face. Behind him, I saw a green flash—like a giant green light from the uni-verse telling us "GO." I later found out it was a meteorite. I saw both it and his face, each lit up with its own celestial energy. He saw only me, his back to the cosmos.

Within a month, he'd stopped speaking to me, finding excuses not to come over, to leave my birthday party after two hours. At fi rst, he blamed me. I'd said something cruel and cold that reminded him of the narcissistic make-up artist. I'd said it in response to a cruel and cold statement of his own. But eventually, when we broke up for good, he said it was not because we had been foolish but because our love had been real. "It's TOO real," he said. "And I'm not ready."

The last time I heard him practice "Big Love," The Barback real-ized he had been playing the whole thing too fast—that, if he'd slowed it down, he was actually pretty good. "But it'll still be a while before I can play the whole thing," he said.

Yes. It probably will be.

In my favorite movie, *L. A. Story*, Steve Martin's character stares out the window at the rain, Enya swelling in the background, as his lover sits staring out her window on a plane, about to leave him. "Why is it we don't always know the moment when love begins," he says, overhead, "but we always know when it ends?"

I love that movie. But I have no idea what he means.

The Barback's turn away from love was so sharp, so sudden, yet the break-up itself took weeks, limping through silences and empty promises to come over and talk and the dark spaces in nights when I'd wake up at 4:00 a.m., expecting him to come to me after work, to come home, night crying dawn with the moon abandoned. The turmoil of his waters created a corresponding movement in my own, not of falling away but falling into an anxiety so foreign, so crippling, I couldn't even wonder what had happened. I only knew something was injured, and I couldn't reach him.

We'd been to a wedding—a fun one, a beautiful one. I'd met his friends. I liked them. They liked me. They liked us together. At one point in the evening, under the paper moon that had hung over the marrying couple, one friend gazed thoughtfully at us. "You two have a really intense relationship, don't you?" she said. It was a statement more than a question. We looked at each other, somewhat startled, but we nodded in agreement. Yes. We do.

We did. How then, could what followed be any less intense?

Certainly, the next day, he was hung over and tired. And the wedding meant he'd see high school friends with whom he'd fallen out of touch, an experience for which he'd prepared, without telling me, before we even left for the ceremony, by smoking up. "Wait," he'd said, touching my arm outside the archway to the event. "I need a minute. I'm super high." A minute is a very long time when one of you is super high and one of you is not—equally long for both, but not equally fun. Though his friends had liked us together, I'd spent most of the wedding trying to make conversation with strangers while he smoked more weed out back, my intense man vanishing and reappearing less present, less intense, each time he'd return. I'd danced to songs I never listened to in high school, and when, as we all waited for our cabs, I reclined wearily on a bench, it was the groom himself, who I'd never met before, who gently patted my head. I wasn't drunk or high—just tired and a little sad. Perhaps a wedding, when we'd been talking about our own as if it were a certainty, made me extra-sensitive to a need for closeness, but that night we simply slept. Then I woke up in the hotel, and he was already gone, out to smoke. And somehow, I felt lonely for the first time in our relationship. I had so looked forward to this weekend, to having this time with him, particularly because his night job made going to sleep at the same time an impossibility and waking up together a rarity. Turning my body to emptiness, I opened my eyes and missed him as if he'd left the continent, instead of just the room.

When he came back, we spent the morning together walking through a Saturday market, and the morning was mostly fine. But the wedding night's beauty was underwritten with those disappearances, the disappointment of waking alone. We were mostly quiet on the drive back, and as he readied himself for work, the seeds of the break-up were sown. "I felt so vulnerable today," I said. I was asking, as we've been told to ask, for what I needed. "Love me up a little extra?" And the face I loved, to which I felt nearly addicted, with all its emotional mobility and sweetness, the face that usually lit up when it looked on mine, this face went cold as an empty bed. "That just seems really insecure."

I wonder if my own face, then, contorted, like the victim of a stabbing, or if it went blank, as when she looks down at her own bleeding body. I had been so sure that he would understand, if not why I was reaching out, then maybe what a gift it is to ask a lover for their hand when we feel underwater—not because we lack the will to pull ourselves out but because it means so much to have someone to ask. I fumbled, trying to explain the difference between vulnerability and insecurity for me. Vulnerability is having the courage to express a need, however irrational it might be; insecurity lurks and is insatiable in its neediness. He saw no difference. Worse, he compared me to the most insecure person he knew, a much, much younger ex-girlfriend. She had known he didn't love her but would ask to be told that he did, which seemed less insecure to me than sadly insightful, a sideways glance at a truth she wanted not to know. The Barback picked up his backpack, turned away, and then turned back. "Why can't I just tell you I love you when I feel like it?" We looked at each other, something like fear welling up in each of us. It was time for him to go to work. I drove him there, and we ran for the tenderness in which fear longs to bury its head. "I love you," I said. "We'll talk." And he still said, "I love you, too," with eyes I still understood. We did talk.

But then, the next night, at a concert, I had too many drinks, and the show was visually chaotic, and he didn't know the music like I did, and as we walked home, I brought it up again.

"It really hurt me that you said I was insecure—I was just trying to talk to you."

"It's kind of Psychology 101 that saying you're not insecure is proof you are insecure."

I stopped and dropped his hand. "Fuck you."

"That moment was the moment I fell out of love with you," he told me two weeks later, two weeks of those nights in the dark. I remembered only that we had been upset but not what I had said, and even if I had, I would have still pushed aside what he had said to me. Nothing said could warrant this departure from my life. We had an intense relationship. That was a good thing, right? I was willing to overlook being told my needs were insecure. And so I had a reaction—people react.

But sometimes that reaction sticks, and that, that is the moment love ends. "That was the moment the chemicals were flushed from my body, and I fell out of love with you."

Is any single sentence more devastating?

Of course, there were other, more significant reasons we broke up, some of which I knew were problems as I rolled over in an empty bed to find him already gone, the need for a cigarette greater than the need to see my face upon waking, than holding me close in the long morning of our first weekend away together. But knowing he had a moment in which he knew his love for me had ended . . . what else could I do for weeks but stare out my window, eyes fixed on that moment which, unfortunately, pushed hazily up from the brain dirt into which it had been drunkenly tucked, the bad seed into the dark earth of memory, bursting suddenly from husk to fully-grown vine? Fast and thick as kudzu, something grew and choked out all the beauty of that love, killing all the goodness like an unexpected frost.

The hardest part about having a break-up song for The Barback is that unlike him and Steve Martin, I have no moment when love ended for me. If I needed to have a moment, perhaps it could be the moment when his lovely face went cold. His face is a serious face and defaults to a frown; maybe it could be the moment when that frown was directed at me. But I don't have a moment, and as I try to recover, it is no surprise to me that the song to which I feel most drawn, the one that seems right, is not a break-up song at all. It is Joni Mitchell's "All I Want," and it is not a song of endings but a song about the desire to love and the difficulties of doing so, an expression of need that is vulnerable, not insecure, because it asks a lover to be with her on a journey towards their better selves:

> *All I really, really want our love to do*
> *is to bring out the best in me and in you, too*

Joni Mitchell asks for recognition of her vulnerability, as I did, even as she takes ownership for her own role in the pain: *Do you see / do you see / do you see how you hurt me, baby? / So I hurt you, too, and we both get / so blue.* But the pain is not the point of the song. The point is that she wants to do so many loving things for this man, *to knit [him] a sweater / write [him] a love letter / wanna make [him] feel better. She wants to make you feel free.*

And that is what makes it my best stab at a break-up song for The Barback, who once wrote me, in his own love letter, that "when something so great becomes so necessary, so quickly, it is NOT unreasonable to ask if it can be forever." His forever ended in a moment, and he stepped off of our path, while I am

> *on a lonely road, and I am traveling looking for*
> *something---*
> *What can it be?*
> *Oh, I hate you some*
> *I hate you some I love you some Oh, I love you*
> *when I forget about Me.*

Real Phone Number, Fake Name: Anger, Music
and (Non)Intimacy

Forget, for a moment, that I met him at a bar. Perhaps forget, also, that Kate and I had met for drinks at 4:30 p.m., and it was 1:30 a.m. when he first kissed me. Because while I've tried to take the blame on those accounts, most of my friends (oh, dear, dear friends) all roll their eyes and remind me of this: "Lots of people met at bars. Bars where they've been drinking. But it is just fucking weird that he gave you his real phone number and a FAKE NAME."

It's not even that dating is getting hard. It's that WANTING to date is getting hard.

The only thing I knew about Nicki Minaj was that she performed under alter egos. I learned this from a student presentation in my British Literature class; she was Lauren's example of a contemporary Oscar Wilde. And I get it: Minaj invokes a character she calls "Roman Zolanski," Minaj's inner "twin brother"—he's "gay," a "lunatic," and he comes out when she's angry. He's the equivalent of Jack Worthing taking on the name of "Ernest" in *The Importance of Being Earnest*. It's the alter ego that enables him (and later Algernon) to court their moniker-obsessed beloveds; it's the alter ego that grants them access to what they want. As Gwendolyn says, "My ideal has always been to love some one of the name of Ernest. There is something in that name that inspires absolute confidence. The moment Algernon first mentioned to me that he had a friend called Ernest, I knew I was destined to love you."

I don't know if I was destined to love Nick From Karaoke, but I liked him an awful lot, and he seemed to like me, too. The VPBB (Very Painful Barback Break-Up) had been over four months ago, and, instead of healing slowly, I found myself angrier and angrier: at the Barback, at myself, and, as a delayed bonus, angriest of all at Elliott.

I *knew* I'd handled that break-up too well.

Some people feel really empowered by anger. As a rule, I don't. And I don't shy away from strong emotions. But the thing I've never liked about anger is that Anger doesn't care about being fair. I can handle righteous anger; I know when to stand up and speak. But the kind I've been feeling is both overly simple and not simple enough. It's not cleansing.

It's my default feeling at night when I can't sleep. It's Elizabeth Kubler-Ross anger—which is to say, it's the anger associated with grieving.

It's the anger I feel when friends don't bother to tell me they've invited Elliott to something, and when I say that I would appreciate a heads-up, I'm told I "should be over it by now" or that I'm only ostracizing myself. It's the anger I felt when he got invited to Passover, and I got passed over. It's the anger I felt when I was promised an Elliott-free Christmas party, in recompense for Passover—a promise to which, I was told, he agreed—only to find he'd asked to be invited anyway, and I didn't know until he walked in the door. It's the anger I'm feeling as I realize I will have to let go of a group to which I've belonged for years because this is my equivalent of a divorce. It's the anger I feel towards him now, as I lose the good feelings I had remaining for him, because he is perceived as someone for whom to feel sorry and I am perceived as unforgiving.

I'd spent a year doing so well: sad but resolute. Better to be without than to remain with someone who couldn't make a choice. And then . . . there was the Barback. There was him and choices made too quickly, my own intuition ignored because it felt so good not to be sad anymore.

And then came the break-up. And then came the anger And then came more anger. So when, at karaoke, a witty, animated, handsome man told me that I "killed it" with my performance of "Back to Black" and asked me for my number, it felt good not to be angry. He texted me immediately, so I would have his number. He told me his name was Nick, and while it didn't inspire the "absolute confidence" of Ernest, at least it didn't inspire any negative emotion. And when he kissed me later that night, one could almost forget sadness and anger ever existed.

That is, until I did what any self-respecting 21st-century person would do the next day. I Googled him. The images that came up for the name he'd given me . . . were not of him. Had I had that much to drink? Nooooo . . . I'd asked if he was a Nickoli or a Nicholaus, and he'd said, "Nicholaus." (To protect the poor man whose identity had been handed over to me, I won't tell you the last name, but I'd been given one. He lives in Germany, just for the record.) He'd told me he headed a marketing firm and dog-sat for a company called rover.com. Well, he doesn't work in marketing—he works at World Spice, behind the Pike Place Market. How do I know? Because he does actually dog-sit for rover.com—and they have a list of their sitters. With pictures. And bios. Real number, real dog-sitter, fake name, fake career. Let's hope he was telling the truth about being divorced.

Reading the bio, and, I'll confess, looking at his Tumblr page, I can see that I would have really liked Chris. (Chris is, of course, his real name—I'll spare you the full name reveal, if only to show I am not wholly lost to dark inclinations.) He is an artist and paints pictures of foxes. I love foxes. He has the *Fantastic Mr. Fox* ON his Tumblr page. He seems silly and wears cool clothes. I am silly. I wear cool clothes. Does it really matter that he lied about his name?

Hell yes. Because what made it ok in *The Importance of Being Earnest* was that Ernest really was Jack's name, in the end—the alias was a surface deception that ultimately had depth. The real person never changed, and the alias wasn't an escape as much as a practice run at being himself. Wilde meant for the play to demonstrate the malleability of identity, but always, at the core, the play is supposed to be funny. Names don't matter if the deception doesn't hurt someone.

Why doesn't this seem funny? Why, in fact, does it hurt?

That night at karaoke, Chris sang Nicki Minaj's "Super Bass," which accounts, I guess, not only for the text he'd sent ("Hey Bryn— this is Nicki Minaj") but also, perhaps, for the choice of "Nick" as alias. The irony is not lost on me now. Somehow, it makes me too sad to be angry—all that hope turned out to be just another trick. Maybe I need to summon up a Roman Zolanski, so someone else inside me can be angry for awhile.

Epilogue

Or maybe I can just be angry at myself.

Quite a while after I wrote this piece, Facebook did what it does best: it shamed me. You know those moments in which it suggests friends for you, based on other friends? I'll bet you do, but I'll bet you don't know how it feels to see Nick _____ suggested and realize you are seeing, in fact, the guy who sang Nicki Minaj, that he hadn't lied, that while he does look a lot like this Chris person you've vilified for your sad little essays, you were the bad one here: obsessive, quick to judge, quicker to write about it and explain away the pain that wasn't even there. What is happening to me with these essays? Am I losing touch with real hearts, imagining overly complicated stories, when simply acting like a normal person and waiting to go on a research-free date would do? *The Importance of Being Ernest*, as you'll recall, is that his name really WAS Ernest all along.

And now I'm wondering who *I* am becoming.

50

Playlist Two

Interstitial Music: Essays on Influence, Recovery and Protection

The Police,
"Message in a Bottle"

The Rolling Stones,
"Complicated"
Doves,
"There Goes the Fear"

Kings of Convenience,
"I Don't Know What I Can Save You From"

P. J. Harvey,
"One Line"

Kishi Bashi,
"I Am the Antichrist to You" and
The Smiths,
"How Soon is Now"

Phil Collins/Marilyn Martin,
"Separate Lives," and others

Teagan and Sara,
"Where Does the Good Go?

Message in a Bottle: Meaning / Mistake

There's an essay called "Metaphor as Mistake" by semiotician and novelist Walker Percy in which he explores the cognitive phenomenon of mishearing a phrase and why that mistake strikes us with sudden emotional potency. For example, says Percy, there was the time when, as a child, he heard an African-American man describe a bird as a "blue dollar hawk." The child was fascinated, believing he apprehended something ineffable about the bird in the name, something evocative, true, specific to him somehow, as an encounter with the divine might be. *I know this moment,* I think, as I read. It's an experience similar to what the poet Gerard Manley Hopkins calls "instress": the moment in which one apprehends what he calls the "inscape" of another being, its innermost self in all its transcendent glory. It is a spiritual moment, Hopkins says, and we only achieve it when our own nature goes out to meet another, a godly namaste, an encounter with pure and perfect knowledge. It is a moment in which love for the world both mirrors and creates love of ourselves. I am a big believer, if not in God, in this.

But then Percy, the child, is told the bird is, in fact, a "blue darter hawk." Rather than a moment of deep recognition, there has been a mistake, a misunderstanding, the older man's dialect slurring the second word into something more mysterious than it really is. Thus, argues Percy, the potency dissipates immediately upon the correction of the error. But, for one moment, the child feels the "truth" of a phrase as if he has bypassed language. And for the moment in which we all make such mistakes, we do: we generate the phrase mostly in our own heads. Metaphor is mistake, both true and untrue—science and poetry, an attempt to assert authority over mystery, to make it closer to something we understand.

In college, my junior year, I fell in love with the first of what would be many Quiet Ones to come. Let's call this one The German Mennonite. It was an uneasy and unofficial relationship: I wasn't Mennonite or German, both of which were important to him, and he wasn't very free, which was important to me. To be clear, he wasn't really German—just of German extract, as are many Mennonites. And if you're still asking "what IS a Mennonite?," suffice it to say you are not alone and that I ended up there because I'd gone to musical theatre camp there and wanted to go to a small school. I wasn't the only one there who'd grown up Catholic; I totally knew the other two. Once, I was told I "believed in a lot of science for a Catholic." I didn't believe in enough, really, to be Catholic or Mennonite—but I believed in thinking hard, which is not really the same as belief or belonging to a culture because of birth.

Still, no one really knows that yet in college, and loving him was my first experience with grown-up love, the kind in which you listen to each other, really listen, without trying to change each other's minds, and respect differences instead of pushing them away. There was, with him, a truthfulness, an attempt to connect deeply that set a healthy precedent for me. It's one I honor still, every time I set myself aside and hear what someone else is trying to say.

But look. See how I go back and forth, even now, the trial of rewriting rejections into peaceable histories? I've made the man a metaphor, when there was so much neither of us could hear at that young age.

The truth: We had always known each other but had never spent much time together. I was a hippie at the corner table, in a broomstick skirt and an over-sized feminist tee shirt; he participated in chapel and wore his shirts tucked in. But then we drove from Kansas to Ohio, spent a weekend together, part of a large group at a wedding. We'd talked more on the drive there than we ever had in three years; there were jokes exchanged and looks. We coordinated our turns driving home so that we were together in the front seat for four hours, talking, listening, asking the questions you only ask in college, when any thoughtful answer might really reshape what you yourself might think. I call it "dangerous listening" to this day.

And this is where the mistake, or love, begins.

The VW bus breaks down—is it surprising this is the kind of vehicle? Or that it breaks down? We talk all night in a 76 truck stop in Troy, Illinois, share stale but free apple pie, snuck to us by Lorna, the waitress, who feels sorry for us or notices how our two heads lean in closer, while everyone else tries to sleep. We talk about God, of course, as you do in college and the dark, which means we also speak of love and art and books that sound pretentious now (*The Stranger, The Foun-tainhead*) but, at the time, are not. They never are, at that time, that age.

Back on the road, we wordlessly seek out the darkness of the backseat, let others take their driving turns. I curl into him; he lets me. I feel the body of this man under my cheek, hear his heart beating so quickly, think I know it now. "Blue dollar hawk," the child hears. I turn my head up to face him, notice how sweetly our lips will fit together. "I can't," he whispers. Blue darter. I lower my face, pretend to be asleep, keep my cheek against his heart, despite its still rapid beating.

Over and over, in the next few months, moments are sensed by me, rebuffed by him: gazes dropped, then resumed, held, dropped again. Sometimes, he comes down to have tea and talk about books. I give up, go out of town, go out with someone else. When I come back, he comes to my dorm room that very night, lifts my face. How sweetly our lips fit together in that first kiss three months after the refusal in the van.

Unlooked for, not sensed by me, these moments come with increasing frequency as his graduation looms. We disappear to sit on rooftops after leaving the bars with friends, talking still, listening still. He learns how bright the moonlight can be upon my pillow. His heart still beats so quickly, and he laughs one night, lying his head upon my chest. "Your heart's beating so quickly," he says, and I kiss his head. The moon hangs like a blue dollar in the sky.

On graduation day, somebody takes a picture in which it is clear my heart is breaking: his arm around me and both of mine around him, his head straight ahead and mine on his shoulder. He is smiling; I am, too, but in that way that means I am about to cry. I wear his blue and yellow flannel, given to me just the night before. It is 80 degrees, and I will not take this shirt off for weeks. One minute before, I meet his mother for the only time, my arms full of irises after moving myself out of the dorms all day. I am sweaty and hot, stained with the ink of all those irises. She puts her arms around me, hugs me close. "I've heard so much about you," she whispers.

Blue dollar? Blue darter? What has she heard? What did he say?

The day he drives away from college, we make out for most of the day. Our faces look again like they did in the picture two days before, but this time he can see my tears. He is going to see a Mennonite girl with whom he thinks he might be more compatible. He isn't, it turns out, he tells me in a phone call, laughing, later that summer. He promises to write, though he promises me nothing about our own compatibility.

He writes me, it's true, the first email I will ever receive, but mostly he writes me letters. Letters—no one raised on email can ever know the fullness of letters from the man with whom you are still in love, no matter what they say, as long as they do not say "no." I am so young, too young to hear that word lurking in every line. Still sharing, still talking. Blue dollar, blue dollar. How sweetly our lips press now the back of each envelope, I imagine.

Pressed on the back of the first is the phrase "Message in a Bottle."

The Police song. It has to be. I told him when he left, my roommates and I watched six hours of their concert videos. What is he saying to me now? I am listening hard again, as I always have. I've heard the Police and liked them, but now I immerse myself in a more intentional Police phase, listening so I can find its meaning for this man. I listen as anyone listens to music when they believe it to be a portal to the mind they love, as if the song is a secret written in many keys and one key will let me in for good, prove that we speak in code, bypass the language to the meaning, recognize the god in me as the god in you. In him.

In the song, Sting is sending out an SOS to the world. He sounds urgent. He must be answered:

Just a castaway,
an island lost at sea
another lonely day
with no one here but me
more loneliness
than any man could bear
rescue me before I fall into despair

I am listening. I sing along: *I should have known it right from the staaaaaaaaaaart.* I sing, knowing what this song, now, really means. And what it really means, inside my head, is this: "I need your love, I need to talk to you because talking to you is love, I need you, I know it at last." And my heart beats faster again, singing it back to him: *Seems I'm not alone at being alone.*

The phone rings, and though this is before caller ID, I know it's him. "Did you catch the reference on the back of the envelope?" he asks. "Yes," I say, my head on his chest in the recesses of my mind, his head on my pillow in the blue dollar moon. "The Police song." "No," he says, "The Bertolt Brecht story, 'Message in a Bottle.'" Blue darter.

⌒⌒⌒

That bottle, then. The German one instead of the sexy one. The bottle: less about belief in me, more about those things so long held dear to him: being German, abstract contemplation over passionate urgency, waiting three months for a kiss while I will always look up in the dark with willing lips, right from the start. I have been wrong. I cannot read his very mind; his heart still beats, but now it is too far across the continent for me to understand him that way.

But I look up the Brecht story again, and in its first lines, I hear myself, and him, and understand at last to whom I have been listening: *I am twenty-four years old. People say that is an age strongly inclined to melancholy. All the same I don't think my melancholy is a reflection of my age. My story is as follows. At the age of twenty I got to know a young man in whose vicinity I felt lighter.* And this young man, who lightens with his presence even in the dark of night, he too abandons the woman. Perhaps it is for someone more compatible, but the reader never knows. For he too gives her a letter, asks that she open it after three years. She waits and opens it, finds, in the end, a blank piece of paper. And the final words of Brecht's story are pure Walker Percy, the muddled intersection between meaning and mistake, between metaphors which clarify and metaphors that simply make clear that only mystery remains:

> *As you know, there is such a thing as magic ink, which is leg-ible for a specific period and then disappears; surely anything worth writing down ought to be written with such ink. I would also just like to add that about a year ago — that is, roughly two years after giving me the letter which is only a blank piece of paper — my beloved disappeared completely from my sight, presumably for ever. After waiting patiently for three years for a message which was less and less meant for me, I can only say that I always thought that love was outside any lover's control, and that it was the lover's business and nobody else's.*

In later calls, he will tell me about his new girlfriend and how important our time together had been to help him engage with her more openly, to appreciate her difference: "I really was in love with you last year, and without that, I don't know that I would have been as open to her." At the time, it made me angry to find that he had come to think of loving me as preparation for loving someone else, and the blue dollar moon had been replaced by the real name of blue darter hawk. Sometimes, I was angry that those letters, those messages, were not an SOS, calling for my help, my love, a recognition of my inscape.

But as I look at us in that photograph, his steady gaze, my own eyes just about to fill, I know there was less mistake and more metaphor. More and more, I see that even before he left, the messages The German Mennonite sent me were never really meant for me. They were for a young man trying to learn about himself, in a language only he really spoke, talking and writing to discover the self he wanted to become. How could either of us listen well when we did not know yet what we most wanted to say? More and more, then, that means that any messages I got from him were messages, somehow, I wrote for myself.

Growing up in western Kansas, my musical preferences were formed on the defense. My high school music came always from the $3 bins, and I am pretty sure I was the only person to own a Morrissey tape in my town. (I will admit now that, at the time, I had diffi culty getting into it—some of the melodies stretched out as fl atly as the plains before me, the warbling urban discontent foreign to my heart, though, intuitively, the wry humor made perfect sense.) I listened to Erasure and Enya, and I took no pleasure in AC/DC, whatsoever. In the 90's, when Nirvana was loud and angry, my college years were devoted to folk music, entirely.

This is the best excuse I can give you for not liking the Rolling Stones for far too many years. This is hard for me to say. If you love music, and you reveal you once didn't love the Rolling Stones, it's like being a dancer and admitting that you really don't like using your left foot. The really wonderful Rolling Stones albums, for me, *Aftermath, Sticky Fingers, Beggars' Banquet,* are big parties, lazy afternoons, and reckless road trips, all in one.

But when I was in high school, the Rolling Stones were "Start Me Up" and "Angie." They were the songs of pot-bellied men past their prime, of street dances fi lled with harvest crews intent on more Coors Light and seducing the unsuspecting high school girl. They were the soundtrack of a life spent in a bar, after a day at a job you didn't love, of dreams not followed or not dreamt at all, of regret. In short, these aging British rockstars seemed to belong to the world I did not love, a world, ironically, "American." (I would make the same mistake about Bruce Springsteen, but I'll apologize for one thing at a time, ok?).

As Fate would have it, perhaps also ironically, the Rolling Stones were gifted to me by a man who, at one point in time, legitimately had an American fl ag up in his bedroom. Non-ironically. This man, deeply intelligent and deadly sincere, is a Mark Twain American: lover of the country, critical of its government. This man, whose full name conjures up an older America (think old-school country and Bob Dylan album titles) likes his privacy, so let's stick with calling him the Mark Twain American: whip-smart poet, lover of music, and one of the only men I know who can pull off a long, Mick Jagger scarf.

My time close to the MTA was a time of critical mass. Twelve years later, I see it as the moment my life turned permanently: without sounding grotesque or pathetic, I want to say it was the last moment to fall in love when everyone else did. All around me, in my late twenties/ early thirties, people were getting married, as if they were adults. I did not know if I was an adult, so when he told me he wanted to marry me, I said, "You think I'm old enough to get married?"

I did not say, "But I already have a boyfriend."

It was about to get messy, painful, but I knew I had a heart to break—because I could feel it hit my breastbone when I saw him. Once, when I asked the MTA if he believed in soul mates, he said, "No—too abstract. I'm more on the side of Aristotle—a heart is only real because it beats." He pulled my hand onto his chest, leaned forward. "And baby, you make mine beat."

Being with the Mark Twain American was one of the most profound and important emotional experiences of my life, which is what made his eventual, necessary, and sharp absence from my life particularly difficult to accept. When I met him, I had no idea what I was getting into. When I see him now, and I do, often (even in large cities like Seattle, writers' worlds are interconnected like conspiracy theory flow charts), I still want to get back in—into that intimacy, that seemingly complete shared intellectual freedom. We are cordial, even warm.

But I made real friendship impossible because I could not make up my mind back then. In the moment I loved the Mark Twain American, there was a window of time, and even then, I could sense that once it closed, it was closed for good—even if I smashed the glass, like a street-fighting man.

I can't say I hadn't been warned. In an email shortly before the first of several ends, the MTA told me my indecision was strangling his love, that though he didn't mind waiting somewhat longer for me to leave my boyfriend, there would come a point at which this thing, which had flared up like a roadside emergency before I could swerve, would no longer grow organically without being fed. And this man who danced drunkenly with me, one night, to "Let's Spend the Night Together," told me this: "Don't play with me, baby," he said, Mick swaggering behind the lines, "'cause you're playing with fire."

Yet, as I think on what I would have changed, how to use that fire as fuel for something good without destroying everything around it, to have allowed friendship simply to be enough, so many moments of insight and beauty would have to go. Walking into the Burke Museum's Shackleton exhibit and instinctively taking the other's hand, free, for a moment, from the eyes of anyone who could know I was a horrible cheater. The list he made me of fi fty things he loved about me (I like Coke, I was born in autumn). The time he took me by the shoulders as I shook with tears, afraid I would be consumed by this love, that I would never be a better person without the infl uence of T he Quiet One, the other man, so much steadier, so unable to move my mind the way the MTA could. "But Bryn, it's you—YOU are the person who makes your-self the person you want to be," he told me. Sometimes, if I let myself look long enough in memory, his warm and cinnamon eyes hold me forever in that moment.

I know I am supposed to say that it was "all worth it." I am now, however, the person I want to be, which means there are moments when the person I was makes me shudder: so crazy, so heedless, so desperate. On some days, I think, if I could, I would give up those moments, if it meant undoing so much pain for three people: the Quiet One, the Mark Twain American, myself.

But if it meant giving up loving the Rolling Stones, I would not do it. Never. I would not change a single thing, unbreak their hearts or my own, and lose "Moonlight Mile," "I Am Waiting," "Factory Girl." I would not lose "Complicated," which the MTA told me, early on, re-minded him of me. In that song, Mick reviews his love affair with a so-phisticate with all the pleasure we take in our own torment: *We talk to-gether and discuss / what is really best for us / She's sophisticated / My head's fit to bust.* In the end, these songs were not the gap between me and America; they were my bridge to it, to an America in which I could belong. I finally heard the longing for connection, not the hopelessness, the rootsy playfulness, not the arrogance. They were not simple—they, too, were complicated. They were British men, in love with the idea that there was more, not less, of joy in the world, and that it was to be found in the Southern rock of another country.

They were, in short, like me: sifting through the music avail-able to them to find the styles that they could use. And they were the soundtrack to a love affair with edges too gritty and hard, too passionate and big, for even the Beatles in their Abbey Road days. I needed music that was rough and exuberant and a little dirty, but sure of what it want-ed, in a time when I was unsure of what I did.

Don't play with me / 'cause you're playing with fire. I was, I did, and I would do it again to bring this music into my life, even as the man who brought it walked away from me, the girl with the faraway eyes.

There Goes the Fear: Sound and Vision

You walk into the restaurant to meet your friend, the one you made when you were dating the man who broke your heart. You ap-praise its clean, streamlined design, and then you see the art on the walls. And it's all by the man whose heart you broke. You know because hang-ing in your own dining room is a giant abstract painting from his more abstract period, before the boat dock period, before that of volcanos. It is entitled "Summer's Gone."

⟋⟍

Abstract Landscapes

You meet The Painter years before you fall in love with him. He is the roommate of another friend; he is the one who sleeps in the bigger closet on the fl oor so he can use the rest of the room to paint. He sits next to you on the couch at parties for two years, near the conversation but not in it. You rarely notice, yet your favorite photograph of yourself from those parties is one he takes: you stand smiling before him, holding part of your enormous red fl amenco skirt above your head so that it forms a whole-body nimbus, your torso in a tight black top the center of this fl ower of y ou, your red hair the stamens.

He asks you to be part of a photography project. He asks you to wear the same red skirt.

You walk up and down Golden Gardens beach while he takes the pictures, a black sweater replacing your party top. He lifts up a rock to show you the tiny crabs underneath. You talk about music, and he promises to make you a mix. By the end, he will have made you fi fteen of them, made you cards, a small book of sketches, taken a hundred photographs, each one showing you in love with this man whose brilliance suddenly crystallizes why you aren't happy with the Quiet One, the bass player. You love them both, but you can talk to him in a way that evades you with the other. There was so much healing and growth after the Mark Twain American affair—you don't want to cheat again on the boyfriend, so you tell them that you love them both, that you need time to fi gure out what you want. They agree to this plan, and you date both for several months. You all learn how to deal with falling in love with multiple people simultaneously, and the lesson you learn is this: you can't.

You know, even as you do it, that it is not the best idea to fall in love while you are still with someone else; "ideas" have little to do with actions, at times, particularly actions taken in because of love. You think love is like his automatic painting technique, in which you make a mark in response to another mark, then another, erasing, perhaps the first mark, until a picture forms that resonates. You erase the first mark and break up with the first boyfriend, but then you erase the second and break up with The Painter, too.

Originally, he calls the painting "Summer's Over," but you kept accidentally calling it "Summer's Gone," and he decides that is sadder, which makes it better. What could be sadder than a summer that's gone forever? The first title is crossed out on the back of the canvas, the mark you left on his art so small on the giant frame, the bigger hearts.

Docks

But you are in love for a long time, before and after it ends, breaking apart only in name, your intimacy synaptic over those temporary gaps. The Painter teaches you how to trust yourself again and shows you how to moor your emotions in art. He has a lot of fear himself, intense social anxiety always on low simmer, making him sweat in grocery lines. But while your fear of making the wrong decision in love paralyzes you, his fear of not producing great works is bigger, nobler, driving him to stay up late into the night, painting, painting, painting, creating, giving fear over to art.

The fifteen CDs, over a year or so, allow you the emotional range you couldn't reach with other boyfriends. The songs are funny and sad and jubilant and true. The Halo Benders' "Don't Touch My Bikini" follows The Cure's "Pictures of You." The New Pornographers' "End of Medicine" and The Arcade Fire's "Wake Up" preface The Postal Service's "Such Great Heights," which you hear for the first time on the surprise road trip to Crater Lake. You are driving and look at him with love in the photo from that same trip, which is on the back of the case of the later mix he makes you with that song.

Because each CD also has its own individual, handmade cover, each a celebration of you and him and love and art. Mix 7 has a photo taken from his parents' porch: a daffodil windsock fluttering in a snowstorm, the dock on the lake just visible in the background, artifice surviving in the face of nature, a strange beauty formed by juxtaposition of unlikely partners. Mix 9 is a collage: the dominant image is a photo of his own bedroom with your cat on his bed from the time he took care of her while you were home for Christmas, but the other images are of your own body, cut into pieces and rearranged. It strikes you now, as you look at it, not that this is creepy and objectifying but rather that it is spot-on, resonating as it did with the divisions you felt within yourself at that time, how he tried to love you for each part of you, to honor the disorder of your many-chambered heart by not trying to put you into a coherent whole when you didn't know what that woman would look like, heart-weary and confused. As if to reiterate your dislocation, on the front of the same mix is a black and white photo of a hand touching a rose, holding it to a face. You don't realize until just now that it is your hand, your own face.

The song you will think of when you think of these safe harbors of song, these gifts of art, is "There Goes the Fear" by Doves. At nearly seven minutes long, it is not a song as much as it is, itself, a collage, an expression of all this love will teach you: the joy and the passion and the commitment to being better, to giving it all away—your love, your soul, your art—because without that giving, enriching those to whom you give, if you withhold it all for fear you will be hurt, you will hold onto less and less. It starts, not slowly, but more gently, a song in which someone helps another locate herself by simply being with her, *out of here, along with fear, as life goes past.* The lead singer's voice is deep enough to inspire confidence, kind enough to pull you closer, enough to *close your brown eyes / and lay down with him.* And then, as you do, the chorus comes, and never stops:

> *There goes the fear*
> *let it go*
> *You turn around and love's passed you by you look*
> *to ones you love to ask them why you look to those*
> *you love to justify*
> *you turn around and life's passed you by passed you*
> *by again*

This chorus repeats with increasing speed and urgency, and the music swells, races like the cars going past in the first verse, a heart racing against the clock to find its own rhythm, to find a way to move past fear, even if it means moving past the other person, just as the singer, in the bridge, gives the other permission to leave:

64

Think of me when you're coming down
But don't look back when leaving town
Think of me when he's calling out
But don't look back when leaving town
Think of me when you close your eyes
But don't look back when you break all ties Think of
me when you're coming down But don't look back
when leaving town today

The song is ocean and shore and waves and boat; it is light sparkling on water, the cold depths, a sea alive with unknown creatures. It is encouragement, forgiveness, hope.

He leaves the painting at your house while you are in Rome, leaving him again, this time for a red-headed architect. Until this trip, you and The Painter have been friends with blurry edges, a friendship built on the hope that you will come to your senses and choose him again. This is a hope on the part of you both. When you return from your summer away, glistening with new love, the summer is over, and The Painter is gone.

Volcanoes

You can think of yourself as his muse, a mystical force that introduced him to the body, to the thrill of knowing that your heart is understood and honored, to the pain of which that heart is capable. You think you have made him more complex. But you are also recreated. He took your passion, your chaos, and rechanneled it into those songs, those drawings, that small book, that art, and you still hang it on your walls because each creation was a reassurance you were going to be ok—not because each piece was about you but because each piece showed you that there was something new beyond all your loss, beyond his heartache.

At Crater Lake, you saw this in the ways destruction preceded regeneration: the barren lava fields on which he laid you like a green plant in your green sweater for a photo, the perfect and pure lake in the crater of a thing that blew its top, the new cone of the volcano, tiny Wizard Island, emerging from the blue, blue waters.

Never get rid of anything he made you. Hang it all on your walls—not because you are holding onto the past, to regret, but because creation, inspiration, and beauty won out against paralysis, numbness, and fear. And because now you know that love exists not just so people can find each other but so that people can make art, make something bigger than the mess we make when we find a love for which we are not ready. And it is that art that makes us fearless—not the foolishness or the triumphs or the pain alone. It is the art that shows us how beautiful it is to feel anything deeply, so much so that we will hang our pain on our walls, put it into our ears and close our eyes and feel protected, bigger, saved.

You stand facing the wall of him in the restaurant. One of the paintings is from his docks period; the other is from his volcano series. There is no abstract landscape, but you know that's where it all began: the eye in search of its own best vision, before those things that would crowd him and crown him until this new series in which fear of geology is all soft colors and hard lines, his own order on those things that move him to create. "I knew him," you tell the hostess before she seats you outside, away from the paintings, and you tell your new friend about this other time you lost and found your heart.

Within 15 minutes, the Red-Headed Architect from Denver turns to me and says, "You want to get out of here?"

"Yes," I say. "Yes."

We are in Rome but have, somehow, ended up in a German bar. We are with students from our respective programs. Though the Red-Head will go on to be an entrepreneur, he is with the University of Colorado architecture program. I am on the UW poetry program. I will go on to be me.

Me right now is escaping my PhD program in Victorian literature—I'm only secretly a poet. I'm secretly uncertain, secretly quite sad, openly a product of a path not known for making smart people feel very smart, after a few years, which is how I've come to spend my social time with the MFA people instead of the other PhD candidates. The MFA students are high drama, love life, stay out late after their readings. Those in the PhD programs have three-hour lunches / grading sessions, worrying about a paragraph and what their director didn't say. My dissertation is on bodies and ekphrasis—the interplay between the visual and the verbal, how images become word, and vice versa, so it is appropriate that my dissertation director is a former theater director versed in spectacle, in making pictures speak. He both adores and torments me, in equal part, the only one who understands my longing to discuss beauty as if it were a value, who doesn't ask me to make my academic work "less lyrical." But, in academia, he is rare. So, I've just finished a full draft of my dissertation, and I want to write poems. I've saved up for this.

Walking back through the Campo di Fiori, we wind through the other pairs of dark-eyed lovers filling the square. They kiss casually, unabashedly, leaning against the statue of hooded Bruno, in the center. Bruno was burned at the stake in the 16th century. The Red-Headed Architect and I are burning in another way. I look at the lounging lovers and feel the flush of recognition I've felt so often this summer.

We climb the endless stairs to his apartment, climb the short ladder to his upper-bunk bed, and lie together, side by side, holding hands. The balcony doors are open, and the sounds of the Campo float in on the warm air, like ashes off a fire. The Architect has the first iPod I've ever seen, and he scrolls through with a touch now familiar to my body. "Here," he says, holding out one of the earbuds," this is a really good song."

In one year, my friend Solange will frown, listening to her voice mail. "What's up?" I will ask. She'll turn. "Did you know I saved your voicemail from New Year's Eve?" I freeze. "Why did you do that?" "Because I knew that you would want to forgive him, and I wanted to make sure that you could remember that you never, never have to forgive him."

I'm versed in forgiveness, attuned to its complexities like a pirate radio frequency wobbling in through thin wires. I've needed a lot in the past four years, what with the affairs and the betrayals—mine and theirs, those poet lovers. I wonder if I'm polyamorous or just indecisive, generous or a monster. I wonder if, like my academic work, my love of beauty makes me unintelligible to others, a weird will-o-the-wisp, a deceptive light for gullible moths. Even as I leave for Rome, the Painter whose heart I've crushed is taking care of my cat. I have forgiven and been forgiven so many times. I want to be better, not to throw myself into something I will have to crawl out of on my knees, a remnant of a temple, desecrated by misuse.

I meet the Architect in Naples, sharing a tour bus and a Belgian tour guide with whom we will drink grappa. The UW poets shame the CU architects by answering all the questions he asks about the city planning as we walk the Herculaneum. When we all stop for gelato, it is so hot the whole group simply stands there silently, the melting sweetness dripping unheeded onto volcanic soil. "I want to marry that guy because of his tee shirt," says Becca, coolly gesturing with her head to the left. He wears a teal Huey Lewis and the News tee shirt, and his hair is shaggy and the most beautiful true red against the green. He looks miserable, sunburnt as only a redhead can be, sweat saturating Huey's face and his own. His long hair drips, his mouth slack. He is stunning in his abjectness, and I move towards him; the heat reduces us to basic impulses, always. "My friend wants to marry you because of your tee shirt," I tell him, bold even in this heat. "Oh, where is she? We ought to get that going." He barely blinks, licks his popsicle, and only then looks at me.

We both like Yo La Tengo, both like *Bottle Rocket,* both miss nachos here. When we return to Rome, get off the bus, I ask him if he wants to go have Chinese with us. At first, he says he'll meet us later, after he takes a shower. But he then catches up to us before we turn the first corner. Later, in bed, he'll tell me, he wanted to go home, recover from the heat, "but then I thought, 'If I don't go right now, I'll never see that girl again'." He pushes my hair off of my face, behind my ear. That girl is me.

Solange hands the phone to me, and I hear sobbing. The sobbing is me. "I am so stupid, so stupid, Solo. I brought this on myself. This was the worst, worst thing I've ever done."

The thing is, I don't believe in saving myself for a future I might have in a place I may not love. You're told, in grad school, you're a martyr to a noble cause, your school debt an investment in the future of what's still not for sale, saving up your joy for a professorship in a small town, with sixteen bars on a two-block radius and not a single man in sight. I'm from Kansas. I've already spent half my life in places I don't love. I'm passionate about my work, but I know what is coming—it's returning to the kind of place I've been. I've been thinking my bar of success is lower, by which I mean higher: living in a city, wrecking my heart, trying to save beauty from the lockbox of school.

But I'm starting to ache. All ruins do, even if they make for good pictures. The Photographer knows that. I don't want to be a beautiful picture anymore. I want to make something.

The Red-Headed Architect and I spend every day together. We give each other assignments to combine our programs: "Write a poem as a triptych with a pediment." "Design a seating area that poses a problem and a solution, like a sonnet." We ride scooters in deadly traffic, nearly dying on a turn near the Janiculum. We walk daily to San Crispino to get gelato and once watch a man propose while standing in the Trevi Fountain. We cheer with the crowd as she steps in as well, boo when the carabinieri walk down to fine him. The lover doesn't care and pays them on the spot. Every lover watching cheers again, and fifty couples begin to make out in solidarity. The rose vender insistently taps our knees with roses, but we are laughing as we're kissing. We are here for this moment, and nothing could be lovelier. We are here, and we are kissing.

I visit Denver and the Red-Headed Architect for the first time only two weeks after our stateside return. When we show up at happy hour with the other architecture students, they are delighted. "What are you doing here?" crows one, hugging me. "Why would I be anywhere but with him?" I say.

I adore him. He is brilliant. We are brilliant together. Each visit, there are more assignments; we like solving problems together. We build our own Hadrian's Villa in his backyard with all the broken door and window frames he's found. We make our own sushi. We go to Casa Bonita, the obscenely pink Mexican restaurant that rises from a strip mall on Colfax. It seats 1000 people, has cliff divers, a Wild West shoot-out, terrible food. "I want to get married here," says the Architect, wrapping his arm around my waist. "Me, too," I sigh. His best friend looks over, cocks his head, says nothing, notes that neither of us said to whom.

"Most people think I'm kind of an asshole," the Architect tells me, as we wait to hear the INXS cover band on the Tiber. Yesterday, he showed me the video he and the best friend made for the band Of Montreal: still shots of pictures from a children's book corresponding cleverly with the lyrics. Today, for class, he designed a bridge based on dancing couples. He shows me how the supports will twist, as if they're arms intertwined. The computer program shows the blueprint, then superimposes the dancers on top. I tear up. It's beautiful. It can be hard to be creative, to not have others understand you.

Graduate school, like most societal enterprises, tells us all we're building a life when we reduce ourselves, narrowing our experience of the present moment to focusing on the future. Instead of giving, we are saving: our money, time, our energy, our hearts. But what of recklessness and the freedom in the process itself, those moments when we are not building but simply being? Rome wasn't built in a day, but it took longer to fall. The falling is the part we talk about—the slow, glorious, lavish expenditure of everything, crashing like a cymbal, its ruins visited like cherished, exotic aunts, who lived their lives so largely that, even in fragments, they are whole.

In the three years after Denver, I am living in a Missouri farmhouse when I get the seventh text. It's been two years since I've seen him. "I'm sorry I wasn't good to you. I'm different now. I can't imagine not knowing you." I try to write the email that will show I take the blame—that I cannot forgive him because I cannot forgive myself. That I was the one who wouldn't see when it was over, that I know changing my ticket to be with him on New Year's Eve was an act of desperation. That, despite all this, it was still humiliating to find he had a date, to spend the day crying until he drives me to the airport. "I may have over-reacted," he says, looking miserable. I see him as he was in Naples on that first day: uncomfortable, detached. At midnight, I look out across the tarmac as the fireworks go off over Las Vegas. I start crying and laughing at the same time, and no one taps my knee to offer me a rose.

I send this email, hoping I have been kind but firm, honest about my pain while owning my part in creating it. He doesn't like it.

"To not forgive is to live in hate. I'm sorry for you, and I'm blocking you from now on."

It's a puzzling response, but this has to end. "Why can't you forgive me? Just because I didn't love you? I always want to know you," he writes the month before. But that's just it: it is just because of that. Because you didn't love me enough to save me from myself.

What is left is what is saved, and what is saved is eternal, like this city. How can we know this, when we build ourselves into structures that stand only because we put them out of reach?

In Rome, the air is thick with spells, the sounds of lovers loving. The Red-Headed Architect puts one headphone in my ear, the other in his own. "Listen to this song," he says. "It's a really good song." There's a sound like an ocean rushing, and my breath catches. *You call me after midnight / It must have been three years since / we last spoke.* Kings of Convenience—I have not heard of them. I had not heard of Of Montreal, which will become my permanent favorite band, who I will love for so long that I will forget who introduced me to them. I had not known such kissing underneath a bridge, my heart beating with that of a city. Later, I will not know such deep humiliation nor understand what kind of friendship can exist after such a mess.

But I do not know it now, and this song is a really good song, this moment one of the best I will ever have in my life, and I know it even as it happens, would know it even if I knew what would be coming. The song advances and retreats: *You changed into somebody / for whom I wouldn't mind to / put the kettle on / Still I don't know what I can save you from.*

What would it mean to be saved from oneself? If one could, who would get to feel the air in this way, like a lover's touch, see the darkness as if the light is only a distraction? If we knew what was next, how terrible the moment, wouldn't we all have to pull away in fear, retreat back to the air as only air? The darkness could only ever be dark, our selves saved but groping in the nothingness. And while nothing is eternal, nothingness is nothing. So then, I hear no warning in the lyrics themselves, will only ever know, when I listen still years later, that I am lucky to remember what I do: the air, the dark, perfection in one moment, the pressure of his hand.

One Line: PJ Harvey and the Cosmos

And I draw a line to your heart today / to your heart from mine / one line to keep us safe. —PJ Harvey, "One Line"

I'm watching from the wall / as in the streets we fight

One definition of Freudian transference is "the redirection of feelings and desires and especially of those unconsciously retained from childhood toward a new object." That is, it's difficult, sometimes, to know if you love someone for who they are or for what they replace: if you love the man or the metaphor, why pain or pleasure from the past becomes a jewelry box, a sweater, an urn. To understand how we redirect our feelings, we have to get some distance, rewind the tapes, and see each event as part of a longer line, a chain in which each link leads us back to the locked compartment of the jewelry box. Pull on the sweater's loose thread. Sift through the ashes for the bone.

This is why, in December of my 43rd year, when I find myself confronted outside of a bar by two angry girls, I'm going to blame alcoholism, I'm going to blame our 45th president, but ultimately, I'm going to blame grief.

To come to such a place as this / you never left my mind.

In 2006, I accept a professorship in Missouri and realize, with terrifying clarity, that I will have to leave Seattle. I'll have to leave natural beauty, craft cocktails, small plates, cute clothes, old friends, large bodies of water, access to the arts, in any form and at any time, the Space Needle . . . . In short, I will leave my life for my career, and it isn't clear to me that the latter will be enough to equal the former.

In 2016, I end an unhappy affair with a man in an open marriage and realize, with terrifying clarity, that I have been alone for too long, that I should try to date again for real instead of spending afternoons in bed with someone else's husband.

Hillary Clinton is running for President, and she would have agreed—I should try. America, however, is making its own strange choices.

This world all gone to war

  I am leaving for Missouri, at the end of July 2006. Knowing this, I begin dating the Skinny Waiter/Writer (SWW in mid-May. I meet him at a friend's birthday party, where I intrigue him, he says, by turning suddenly to him and feeding him bites of his own enchilada without asking his permission. He is ridiculously funny, mostly very smart, and so terribly tall/bone-thin that I think of Don Quixote every time I see him—the stylized silhouette of a dreaming man. We go swimming every day, listen to music, laugh very hard.

  It is roughly July of 2016 when I start seeing the Alcoholic. I meet him at a show while on my second internet date with someone else. I meet him, tellingly, in line for drinks. My date leaves early, and the Alcoholic sidles up next to me. "So, is that guy you were with gone for the rest of the night?" "Yes," say I. "Do you want to go outside and make out with me?" "Yes," say I.

Do you remember our first kiss?

  SWW and I swim every day in Magnuson Park, minus a three-day lull, in which I wonder what is up. Texting me to meet at the beach, we swim as usual, and as we lay side by side, I in my bikini, he turns to me, anxiety and embarrassment in his narrow face. "Brynny, I love, love, love hanging out with you, and I think you are so wonderful and so smart. But I'm not sexually attracted to you." There is a very specifi c kind of vulnerability when you're broken up with in your bikini, by a much younger man who once, in a short story where you are clearly the female character, describes your body as "a child's drawing of a wom-an—all eyes and breasts." Shame suddenly drips from your body like lake water, the swim towel suddenly not big enough to hide your aging, imperfect, suddenly undesirable frame.

  But by the end of that same night, we cry, drink a bottle of whiskey, make love, and resume it all. Mysteriously, the Skinny Waiter/Writer brushes off that afternoon, says he wants to be with me for the rest of my time in Seattle. More mysteriously, although perhaps not, given my own fragile state, we do. We have a wonderful summer, tinged always with my impending loss of the waters in which we swim.

  That first night, The Alcoholic and I talk until 4:00 a.m., at which point he tells me directly he's an alcoholic and that he hates himself. He gives me his number, a kiss, a wry smile, says he might get back together with his old girlfriend, but he might not. The pain of the affair with the man in the open marriage flares, and I remember how to see the red in all the flags before me. I delete his number.

Then I add him on Facebook. It is as if I need to suck more blood from my own wounds.

He calls me once to pick him up, three or four weeks into dating. Later, I will realize it is from the ex-girlfriend's apartment. A month later, I go to my liquor cabinet and pull out an empty bottle. Then another. And another. I walk, ten empty bottles filling my arms, into the living room where the Alcoholic sits on the couch. "What the fuck?" I spit.

Donald Trump is running an aggressive, hateful, confusing campaign. Confusing, I guess, if you don't let yourself understand why he is doing what he is doing, if what is happening seems so unreal you could almost pretend it isn't real life, isn't happening.

To come to such a place as this

The night before I begin my move to Missouri, the Skinny Waiter/Writer and I go to Golden Gardens beach. I do not know my move will be temporary, that I will not be able to stand being away from this city, much less this magical beach, which is scattered liberally with glass hearts for the weeks after Valentine's Day. We split a bottle of prosecco and the earphones to an iPod. In one of his more boyfriend-y moments, he puts his sweatshirt on me, since the night is cool. We hear another couple making out nearby, and we can't stop giggling. Then we are silent for a long time with the stars, and PJ Harvey fills the darkness, filling it like the tide coming in, like sadness in a heart: *Do you remem-ber the first kiss / stars shooting across the sky?* Because the beautiful moments in life are a combination of the unreal and the very, very real, we see, in that moment, a shooting star. And Skinny, who is not as in love with me as I am with him, gasps, grabs my arm and kisses me.

The Alcoholic is lovable, when he isn't making himself into an object, a void. He paints small pictures and loves my cat, who loves his unwashed and boozy smell. He calls me Honey, suffers real pain. I have no experience with addiction, have no idea what is coming, how phone calls will come from unknown numbers to tell me where his beaten body

74

is, how his phone will light up with texts from other women, how I will look, then look away, then say something, then let him stay in my house. I am teaching a class on empathy and feel I have to help him when he can't sleep on the couch of a friend anymore—he's been sleeping there a year—so I let him move in, temporarily. I meet each bad thing like some oddity scrolling across the bottom of the feed of my life. I think the real story has to be somewhere else, a real jewel in a box.

A recording is released of Donald Trump, in which he claims both no responsibility and great power. "I can't help it," he says. "Grab 'em by the pussy—you can do whatever you want."

You never left my mind

It isn't "goodbye" because saying goodbye to the Skinny Waiter/Writer would mean saying goodbye to Seattle. Alone in a new town, in a house by myself, I learn how to chat online, make him CDs and packages and write him beautiful letters. He does the same, sends me mix after mix after mix with songs like David Byrne's "She Only Sleeps with Me" and the Tindersticks' "Sweet Memory." He visits in October; I spend a week with him during Christmas break. I think he means it when, on a tearful drive to the airport, Sufjan Stevens's "Romulus" playing, he stares ahead and says, quietly, "I love you."

The Alcoholic is visiting his family in 2016 Indiana Election Night, and we stay on the phone until dawn, miserable and bewildered. We cry for the country and out of shame we didn't see it coming—our own illusions about our own power suddenly lit up like an electrical fire, like burning ships. "I just want to be home with you," he says. "You get it."

You were the only one / who could have brought me here

The Skinny Waiter/Writer breaks up with me in January. We don't yet know I will quit this job after two years and move back to Seattle. But even if we did, it would not have stopped the future from running away from us towards its own mysterious places. I learn more about how to be alone in Missouri in more sustainable ways: more, that is, than waiting for a future with someone who is really just a container for my past, the urn for the ashes of my old self.

The Alcoholic and I are outside of the bar in December when the two girls march angrily up to us. They glare at him, then turn their eyes on me. One looks humiliated, but the other vibrates with rage. "So, are you two dating? Are you dating?" The fury in her voice is that peculiar to a woman scorned. Hell hath no such fury, nor such scorn as that in those words or the next, after I say yes. "But you're poly, right? You're open?" "No," I say, my escape from this moment and this relationship opening before me like a terrible dawn cracking the sky, an urn smashed to the ground. The Furies turn on the Alcoholic, and I know where he might have really slept during my mother's Thanksgiving visit. "I'm going to go," I say, and walking to my car, I vibrate with the return of my real self, a reality I recognize, even if I'll be alone, even if that reality wobbles like a mirage before me.

In two days, it will be one month since the Election.

One Line to Keep Us Safe

I quit the job and get myself back to Seattle. I kick The Alcoholic out. I believe the presidency of 45 will end.

But I survived the grief of losing my city, then my country, because of these men who both did and didn't love me. They were there when it hurt, and we shared something, even if the edges of those loves were always dark.

But was it me, or the moment? Was it him, or him, or the way both embodied a time in which I could still speak? Were we trapped in an illusion, an unsustainable past, or did SWW or The Alcoholic, too, need me to let him know he had a future? Does it matter which "him" I mean? Sometimes, grief pushes us outward because what's inside can't make sense of itself. We need to see how unreal the object is before us, the one we thought could help us keep everything we loved: a city, a man, a sense of self, a country in which another's suffering matters. But maybe "sustainability" is just about sustaining a state one can accept for the moment. And, if we don't stay there forever, maybe it's ok that transference helps us get to that state. The Skinny Waiter/Writer, the Alcoholic, 45—they're all synecdoche for something much, much harder, something one can't tackle as a whole.

But what was I to them?

I'm on the first date, a picnic date, with This Charming Man. It was the name of The Smiths cover band we met at a week ago, and my friends like to give all my dates nicknames for easy reference later. ("How was the Train Conductor?" they ask. "Busy—he really DID work on the railroad all the live-long day.") This Charming Man and I lie in the grass of the arboretum, splitting an iPod and a bottle of wine. "Here," I say, "listen," and Kishi Bashi plays, the clouds racing like microfiche across the sky. Charming closes his eyes and holds my hand.

"I like it," he says. "There is so much music I wanted to see with you this summer."

I am already cranky. Of course we meet just before he leaves for six weeks in Europe. This moment—the music, the hand-holding, the wine, the air—this is what I wanted for the rest of the summer. And I'm not going to get it.

"Six weeks isn't really the whole summer." He smiles at me, rolls over on his side to touch my face. "And there's lots of music we can go to in the fall."

That sounds like a promise of dates to come, but I am good at hearing what I want to hear. My couples therapist told me so, a year earlier, as I sat on the couch with Elliott and realized our long-term relationship was over: "Bryn, he's not saying no, but he's not saying yes. So, why do you still hear maybe?"

I am so afraid to be on this date, afraid I will feel something and he won't, or that we will both feel something and I will do all the work, or, worst of all, that I will feel nothing—not because I don't like him but because I understand, finally, why dating and skepticism have come to be bedmates, why one goes through the motions without hope of something more. I am trying so hard to let this date be just that—one date. Followed maybe by another. Maybe I'll hear from him when he gets back. Maybe I won't.

He spends an inordinate amount of time explaining how he's usually over-committed and how he could only see the last girl he dated once a week during the school year, between graduate school and teaching. He seems honest and thoughtful, but what's a girl supposed do with all the caveats? I look at him sideways. "Why are you on this date, then?" Charming looks startled. "Why not?"

This doesn't really explain why he is giving me so much backstory on how little to expect. The night we meet at the Tractor, sometime during "How Soon is Now," he tells me he always tells girls two things before he asks them out: 1) that he doesn't have any money and doesn't care about it and 2) that he isn't ready to have children. Do people not even use lines to attract one another anymore? Although he is from California, this seems so Seattle. "So, you're asking me on a date?" I ask. He kisses me, and we go back to dancing, singing as if "now" is soon enough.

I can overlook a lot when singing because I love music. I love it so much. I plan my days around how to fit more of it in, sit down once a month with my daily calendar to look through all the venue listings, make lists of shows I want to go to, console myself in traffic with playlists. When I like someone, I have to hold myself back from making them a mix after each date. I want to make them mixes more than I want to have them over for dinner.

I want to make him a mix.

I want to make music about him.

And I am out of practice.

But you know how I practice music? I don't practice.
I sing a lot, loudly, in the car and in my home, serenading my cat Judy and perfecting my Joni Mitchell octave jumps.

But I haven't picked up my guitar in three years.
When I do, it's all I want to do. I leave the guitar for so long it feels like a recession, a financial crisis where everyone has to develop new skills to face a changed world, for so long that it feels like rejection. I won't play for so long you'll think I forgot how or that I must not want to anymore.

And then, I'll pick it up, and that's all I want to do for months.

What if I pick it up—pick HIM up—and he's all I want? If I am not all he wants? But you don't always practice in order to "get" something. You practice because you love being there: with the music, the man, or because you know it's good for you. I've spent years trying to become more disciplined. In high school, I played both flute and piano, and while more diligent about piano than flute, I still had to trick myself to maintain the regime, to promise myself ice cream if I did 50 minutes or to remind myself how much my mom loved hearing me practice while she made dinner. As a child, I tried the tricks suggested in my mother's ancient piano books: balancing quarters on the tops of my hands to keep them even and arched (very hard) or following in the footsteps of Mozart, who would start over entirely every time he made a mistake (very maddening). Practicing was rarely something I did for myself, really, and that's why, despite my performative inclinations, I can't imagine being a musician for a living.

Charming Man and I lie in the grass, and I want him to kiss me and tell him, so he does. But then he tells me he wants to move more slowly, and I feel, again, my lack of discipline. How uncomfortable to wait—not to use the power a kiss gives a spell, to practice patience. Do I even want to know this song, I think, without a question mark, the way my students write their questions in papers, sidestepping genuine curiosity for the easier way out.

Charming feels my sudden disinterest, looks at me, hand on my face. "I *am* interested. This is how I show I'm really interested—to want to get to know you more," he says. I wonder why it's so hard for me to re-imagine slowing down as anything other than the slower death of passion.

Why? I think I know.

Practicing music, for me, has a side effect. My real passion is language, love of words, and you know what I don't feel like doing when I'm in a guitar spell? Writing poems. Considering the arc of an essay. Explaining myself. Even when I've been writing songs, somehow, the immersion into one universe seems to require that I exit the other.

In language, I know myself and I can reach out to others.

But when a guitar fit comes over me, I leave language. My fingers cramp into their old positions, the F chord frustrates me more than waiting for a second date, the pads of my fingers develop callouses more quickly than my heart. I practice and practice the same songs until I can sing and sing them, walk down a chord as easily as walking down the block. I play and play without thinking, without considering where I'm going.

So I never really get any better as a musician. The songs I know are passionate but simple. It's the same stuff I already know, and waiting is not what I know, and I don't know if I can learn this song. I don't know if I want to learn this song.

Sometimes, I feel like this is me as a lover: returning over and over to the same songs, the same four chords. I wince to think of how I will have to develop the callouses all over again, wish I could break my old habits and learn better, more sustainable ones, improve as a musician and a woman.

But practicing for others is something I don't do anymore, and maybe I still don't do it for myself. Maybe this is just how I do it: I pick up the guitar, I fall in love, after long absences from both, and that's all I do for awhile—not so I can get better but because the feeling comes over me, and it's what I want. And when I'm good enough at the basics to sing along, I sing and sing. And it is glorious.

But that's a bit self-congratulatory, isn't it? Aren't songs meant to be sung with other people, mindful of their rhythms, of the adjustments needed for their range and their abilities?

Charming Man is packing up the picnic. I wonder if slowing down might be, perhaps, a way of keeping myself in both language and music: both clarified understanding and blinding immersion, the sense of fully connecting with another while getting into that broader space beyond myself, the one I feel in music. What would it feel like to get to know someone gradually, building up to the bar chords, still bursting jubilantly into the chorus?

I don't want to think of "going more slowly" as an "improvement" on my way of loving. I like my way of loving. I like to sing and sing and sing.

But maybe it's hard for someone to stay in that song with me. Maybe it's not fun to feel like you're just the back-up singer, never in charge of any verses. Maybe my way of falling in love feels more like being put under a spell than creating something together. Maybe that's why Charming resists my magic. Or maybe, he's asking me to do something new, something that involves choosing to practice differently.

I have had a lifetime of getting to the good parts—not because I can't do the hard work but because I know how to get to the good parts quickly. What would it feel like not to know the song at all, not to know when the good parts were coming? How will I hold on until they come? What if I practice and practice and never get any better? What if I practice and the good parts never come?

We walk back to the car from the picnic, holding the picnic basket between us, one handle per person, and I joke that I want this picnic to be a "collaborative effort." I am jittery; this must be what people feel when it's been just a good date, instead of magic: all tension and uncertainty, but pleasant. I have only his word that he wants to see me again. Having asked him a lot of questions today, I ask him to ask me one. Charming turns his head, looks intently at me, asks it. "You seem really good at making magic happen. How do you do it?"

I could tell him how I am like the many-chambered nautilus,

heaving my whole body into the room of each new relationship. I could tell him each lover is a new song for me to master, to practice and practice until their words have lost all meaning and they are purely sound. I could tell him I burst forth so jubilantly, others think they are the star on stage. But I have to make a new space, even if it means I'll break what remains of any spell I might be casting.

"Well," I say, slowly, "a lot of people tell me that I'm magical. They say it's in the words I say. But really, I think it's the opposite. I'm trying to ask the right questions, and I care about the answers. I'm willing to wait to hear your words. I guess most people don't get that enough— to say their own right words. I try really hard to hear them." He nods, as if this is answer enough for now. It probably is. But, inside, I hope there is more time with him, more time to practice, even if it doesn't make this connection, or me, perfect.

During high school, I drove myself each week to piano lessons thirty minutes away, in another town, and reflected on being and nothingness. There were no towns in between my town and that town. There was a feedlot and some scattered roadside farmhouses and a lot of time to think about the relationships I had not yet had. Although it was the early 90s, I was listening, on tape, to SO MANY 80s love songs. Favoring soundtracks, I'd argue the 1985 "Love Theme from *St. Elmo's Fire*" is a solid template for most of the songs informing me at that time: a song of lost love, nostalgia for a time gone by, or simply the pain of growing older, time passing as we speed towards death. Others of its ilk includ-ed "Separate Lives" (also written in 1985, but in the 1990 film *White Nights*) and a song called "When She Danced" from a 1988 movie called *Stealing Home*, which I watched obsessively on HBO, every time it came on.

I was sixteen. What did I know of love at all, much less love lost? I was always moving towards pre-emptive nostalgia, missing the thing before it had happened. Did all those songs prepare me for the worst or encourage me to let go too soon?

I want to believe they trained me in empathy, pulling me out of my teenaged emotional self-absorption into a relation with the break-ing adult hearts of Phil Collins or Marilyn Martin. I could feel that for which I didn't yet have words or even life experience. Someone was in pain, not my pain, yet for each mile passed, each song sung, a sixteen-year-old grew old and wise and thoughtful alongside another's tragedy. If you watch the "Separate Lives" video on YouTube, you'll find a lot of comments that indicate there may have been a whole posse of prema-turely world-weary teenagers feeling the same way. One man notes this "sad fact: 'When you're happy, you enjoy the music. But when you're sad, you understand the lyrics.'" And I guess someone named Vickie Clarkson and I would be friends because she "remember[s] listening to this at 15. I'm now 45 and it's still brilliant."

There's an incredibly moving *This American Life* episode called "Dr. Phil" in which Starlee Kine decides to try to write a break-up song and calls on both the keyboardist from the Psychedelic Furs and Phil Collins to help her. The Psychedelic Furs are cool, you think, but why Phil? Because, against all the hipster odds, his songs had become her songs. Kine says:

> *I don't quite remember how our Phil Collins phase began. I think it was one of those things that started off ironically, with Anthony lip-syncing, adorably, to "Against All Odds" one night. But over time, it became less and less ironic, until one day, we were actual fans. [. . . .] We liked how honest and sad it was. How can I just let you walk away, just let you leave without a trace? You're the only one who really knew me at all. We pictured Phil Collins at the piano writing it, the tears running down his face.*

Take that in: they could picture him, with tears running down his face. In their interview, Phil Collins tells her "Against All Odds" was written about his divorce. He so easily and generously compares Kine's painful, but relatively less life-changing break-up to the restructuring of both his career and his family, all the while never making her seem silly or lesser. Quoth Phil:

> *There are various people in your life that you never quite get over. I mean, that's kind of the cliché. And then sometimes, with me, for example, because of children, you are morally obligated, and if you want to be with the kids as much as possible, you have to be in touch with this person that's really hurt you. So it's not like you can just walk away and leave without a trace because, in this instance, there's a couple of little guys that are looking up to you, saying, what am I going to do, Dad?*

But the moment that kills me, that teaches me the most about empathy, is when Starlee Kine plays her break-up song for Phil Collins and, after discussing the song's quality itself, she timidly asks, "Do you think he'll come back to me?" And Phil Collins says, earnestly, kindly, "I hope so."

You might argue that songs like Olivia Rodrigo's "Driver's License" also educate teenagers on nostalgia, but that's a more traditional nostalgia, a yearning for what a teenager might have already known and experienced. I often wonder if teens are given the freedom and space, in this era of narcissistic self-care, to really get outside of themselves. I'm told the internet makes the world so big for them, but there are also a lot of ways you can curate your experiences online to reflect back only yourself: to find only what you think you want, think you need, or think you like.

I watched *Stealing Home* only at the times it aired on HBO, sometimes staying up until midnight to catch it again, and I watched it repeatedly because it was what was available to watch, other than reruns of *Hogan's Heroes*. It wouldn't seem, perhaps, like a movie to which I'd be drawn, but it was something to do on a 100- degree day in Kansas[2]. Mark Harmon is Billy, a deadbeat living in a motel, when he gets the call that his childhood babysitter, Katie (Jodie Foster), has killed herself. He goes home and is told Katie left him in care of her ashes, that he would know what to do. We go backwards and forwards in time, learning about his world with Katie, what hopes they had, what problems were already coming, and witnessing adult Billy's attempts to make sense of his downslide in relation to his disconnection from his old life. "I've been one lost son of a bitch," he tells his high school best friend, who is, himself, trapped in a loveless marriage.

What made me watch it again and again was empathy. You watch fi rst perhaps because something is before you, but if y ou stay present for it, there's a glittering shift from curiosity to connection, from a passive external witnessing to an active internal recognition that this, too, could happen to you. It's the same phenomenon I experienced when I first watched *Death of a Salesman* my freshman year of college. I cried all the way back to my dorm. "It's just a play," said my roommate, who'd also watched it and was unmoved. (She's a litigator now.) "But that could happen to us," I sobbed, wiping my eyes on my book bag. "We could think we're doing fine but be tricking ourselves." Ultimately, in Stealing Home, adult Billy has to get beyond his own problems and to reflect on what Katie would have wanted. In doing so, by the fi lm's end, he also comes to understand what he might want again for himself. A key scene in this conclusion is his remembrance of the one and only time he and Katie made love, during which the song "But When She Danced" plays. While Billy's virginity is lost in an earlier, comedic scene to a girl he barely knows, it's clear that, with Katie, he is with someone who not only loves him but knows him, as well as he will ever be known. Katie leaves teen Billy the next day, telling him to stay focused on his talents in baseball, before vanishing forever. Sound like any other 80s songs you know? The movie itself is basically a song of its era: nostalgia for a time gone by, the pain of growing older, time passing as we speed towards death, or, as in this movie, the death of others.

---

[2] The Quiet One completely blew my mind once by breaking out into the rap "Top That" from the HBO movie *Teen Witch*, another movie I'd watched repeatedly on hot summer days. He grew up in Minnesota.

As I sped past empty fi elds on my way towards music, the music in the car fi lled those fi elds with sunlight, made them full of what I could not see or even yet imagine: large-scale emotional failure, dreams not just deferred but betrayed, the inevitability of endings. There are so many words out there for our feelings. The Welsh have *hiraeth*, defi ned as "the yearning for something that cannot be experienced, attained or completed. The piece of music you won't hear, or the garden you'll never visit. Perhaps a person you won't ever talk to, or a someone who never existed at all." The Germans, of course, have a word: *sehnsucht*, "a yearning and longing for alternative, ideal experiences." But is there any better word than empathy for those feelings I had in the car, as I listened to others' stories? Is pain ever "ideal"? Wouldn't I feel the same way, even if I was or wasn't going to have those same experiences later? I couldn't feel death at sixteen, but I could approach how someone else might feel. And I learned that you could survive it.

Marilyn Martin sings on both "Separate Lives" and "When She Danced." She is also the wailing background singer on Tom Petty's "Don't Come Around Here No More." She's a real estate agent now. If you continue to read the YouTube comments for "Separate Lives," many people ask why Martin didn't become a bigger star. Maybe singing these songs prepared her to know how to throw all of herself into another's lyrics, to sing alongside a moment not hers and create something glow-ing, without expecting it to last.

You Remind Me of the Babe: Labyrinths, Tegan and Sara, and Go ing Nowhere with Love

"That is what I HATE about American Buddhism," my friend Sonora says. "Everyone thinks they're detaching to GET something, instead of just BEING."

It's true—we even need to make NOT getting, not going, a kind of getting and going. It's "growth," it's "moving towards enlighten- ment." My favorite Buddhist saying reflects the futility of trying to make meaning of one's own growth in the moment it is happening: "Oh, my friend, going in circles—you may enjoy going. But not in circles."

So the saying . . . goes.

As much as I hate the name "Tegan," smacking as it does of made-up sorority girl names, there is one Tegan and Sara song I think of, with terrible regularity: "Where Does the Good Go?" Its chorus refuses Buddhist detachment and demands an account of feelings remaindered like unpopular books: "Where does the good go?" While other clever lines clarify the singers' losses, what sticks out is simply the repetition of this refrain, always calmly, as if it were not a desperate statement.

I often pass, while on my way to work, a church with a bulletin board that periodically invites you to walk its labyrinth, an invitation to meditate while walking, meeting obstacles as they come.

Is that labyrinth, too, supposed to "go" somewhere? Or are you just supposed to know, with each false turn, each dead end, that God is waiting in the center? Or is he/it walking with you, "Footprints" style?

I make no claims to believing in any guiding force, but I don't mean it as a theological (or anti-theological statement) when I say I'm coming to think of Love as a labyrinth with neither Minotaur nor Goblet of Fire in the middle. (And, frankly, if you'll recall, the Goblet of Fire itself was actually no prize but a trick, a monstrous, deadly trick of a portkey.) When the obstacles aren't glaringly obvious—red flags of ivy and of thorn (he has no career! he has no hope!), they seem to grow up in front of you, almost of their own accord, Harry Potter-style, with no purpose but to block your way. "Try again," they whisper, and so you turn around, try to remember which routes you've tried and which you still have left.

Is this growth, this retreading of old ground? Is my writing, with its obsessive reconfigurations of the past, the story-boarding of my life with an ever longer soundtrack, a discography of singular moments of intimacy and B-sides of my heartbreaks . . . is it growth? Or are these several loving walks down Memory Lane ending, again and again, with the same sign at the end: Trail ends here. Turn around.

Where does the good go? The literary soul in me feebly makes the case for Roethke's claim that "we learn by going where we have to go." But that, too, turns all that desire, the deep pleasure in a former loved one's face, the feeling of their hand in the dark, into a roadmap going somewhere—turns all that glorious love into mere accumulation, the shadows of some greater "There."

In a movie from my childhood, *Labyrinth*, David Bowie plays the Goblin King and talk-sings a little ditty with some now-forgotten creature:

> *Bowie: You remind me of the babe*
> *Creature: What babe?*
> *Bowie: Babe with the power. Creature:*
> *What power?*

In that labyrinth, the search is for the thing you think you didn't love until it was taken away from you. In this one, this writing of my own emotional maze, its hedges taller every turn, I sometimes wonder if that's what I'm searching for, too—as if, somehow, by revisiting myself as the babe with or without power, I could find out where the good goes.

Box Sets

Box Set: A History of Us in Debt
       Liz Phair, *"Supernova"; Sting, "Fields of Gold";* Tori Amos, *"Father*

            Lucifer"; Beck, *"Lost Cause"*
  What Is the Light?

    Five weeks of radiation CD mixes, various artists

A History of Us in Debt

The Short-Term Loan

You are 12, and I am 16. We are at musical theatre camp, and you are the real performer, lying about your age so you could attend. You see one long braid down my back and follow me around, from the cafeteria to vocal rehearsal to dance practice, where you want to be partnered with me, as if you could spin my red hair into gold. I think you are 14 and only notice you because I believe I am worth following and because your eyes unsettle me, watching me as a cat watches unseen souls in the darkness. Because of the age gap, I feel powerful, but when you first touch me, I become a liquid asset, transfigured by your heat into something altogether different. There is kissing behind the sets and on the stairs to the dressing room. You call me once that year and talk about horror movies, which I find disgusting, and you seem both arrogant and naïve.

At camp that next summer, and for the next five summers—even when I am in college and your counselor—we will continue to withhold affection spitefully, the age difference an arrogance of its own. The withholding takes different forms: one year, you will awkwardly ask me, at the beginning of the week, if I mind that you want to be with some other golden-haired teen beauty who can tap dance. The next, I will mock you for your devotion; I will do this cruelly to prove that I am learning something in college, until my fellow counselor, who is also my best friend, who is also in love with me, will yell at me outside of the dorms when our campers—including you–sleep inside because I never look at him the way I look at you.

So then, each year, each of those weeks will end with our reunion, magnetized to each other by doubt and conflict. We will give in, give it all to each other in those moments when we feel time running out and the rest of the year, after one summer week, spreading out like a certificate of deposit. Our touches feel grasping and greedy, but our tears and our silences are ever plentiful and free. You will tell me that you love me, and our weeping is a consecration. We are like a young married couple applying for our first loan—the loan to buy our dream house. We do not know that we cannot afford this house, nor that we will pay for it for the rest of our lives.

Legacy

You are 18, and I am 22. We make love once—my first time—that June, at camp, of course, although this time, I have had to drive to meet you, no longer even a counselor, for you have called me, extracting the number from a college friend still working on campus. You have called me, and I must come because there is an uncashed check in your voice, and I must sign for it. When you walk out of the choir room and see me, you stop, radiant, and I ignore the greetings of all who still know me, pushing past them to bury my face in your warm hair, your neck, the secret of us revealed to all around like a legacy read off by an executrix. That night, your roommate sleeps in the current counselor's room, since the counselors now were campers who knew Us, who knew about the dark walks after rehearsals and me coming back in tears, you flushed with lust and confusion. This roommate will have told you not to call, that one's best chances are with girls one's own age; however, since I have shown up, he is impressed, sets his bar higher, and sleeps on the floor in the next room. I have been naked before with men but never with you and never for sex. We have never had more than an hour alone to count the prizes among the treasure of our bodies. For years, I will tell others that the song playing was Liz Phair's "Supernova," but it is, in fact, "Fields of Gold" by Sting, in stark contrast to the bare walls of the dorm room, made stranger by my knowledge of the room's previous inhabitants, how the walls, during the school year, were covered with a dime store tapestry and posters of French films. It is harder to accept this gift than I thought, though neither of us doubts that it is time for it to be given and received.

This is your last year attending camp. You will go to Colorado the next, intending to study film; in two years, you will have a son you did not plan. You will drink your twenties away, hoping that merely staying near him will make up for your own father's disinterest. But now, you are 18 and I am 22, with an entire night before us. I wear your dead grandfather's robe to the bathroom in the middle of the night, and your roommate tells you that you have eaten of the forbidden woman.

Bankruptcy

You are 18, and I am 22, at a Best Western in Tulsa, a city I do not know at all, in which I have little interest except that it holds you. It is the second hotel room I ever pay for by myself; it is the first for these purposes. I have driven all day to Tulsa, your home, where I have never visited you, simply because it did not occur to me that I could, our assets so tied up in location, so rooted in camp. It occurs to me now because I have a paycheck that isn't from work-study, which somehow legitimates this plan. It later occurs to me to wonder why money legitimates anything about being grown up.

It is one in the morning, and I have been here since eight o'clock, watching the television and wondering when you will come home and find the message I have arrived, despite the fact you knew I was coming. These are the days before cell phones, when one had to trust in the goodness of mothers to pen a note from the girl she knows you love and have no business loving. One hopes the recipient notices the note on the counter, in the dark, when he returns from a night out with friends, doing the things that lead him to rehab years later. Tori Amos, your idol, is on *The Tonight Show*, singing "Father Lucifer." She wonders if Joe DiMaggio still puts flowers on Marilyn's grave. I have been wondering many things. You arrive, and I think of nothing to do right, over think everything else. We are in bed again, for the second time, and I do not know why I have to get up and leave the room for a minute, after sex, but it has something to do with the division of this room from this situation, of myself from you.

The next day, at your parents' home, you say you do not know fully for what I have come, which makes two of us, since this was a gamble, an unsound plan with unstable backing. You tell me it is too strange, that you have nothing to give me, that I will always be the gold standard for women, but all we have given is foreign currency, beautiful and worthless: it cannot be exchanged for anything, except at a reduced rate, and will best become a trinket. When I return to my apartment that night, I play "Father Lucifer" on repeat one; it will repeat for two weeks, as I lie on the floor and drink cheap wine, getting up only to teach my composition class.

But that is after the drive home, which takes four hours, so I will cry all the way back to Kansas and throw change into the tollbooth every thirty miles, until I have nothing left.

Refinancing

You are 28 and I am 32. I have made a huge mistake, moving from Seattle to Missouri, and I am alone in my office when I receive your message on Friendster, reading, simply, "Just let me explain." On the phone that night, we talk for the first time in eleven years. We talk as we never have or could when we did not understand the value of even our own lives—the many ways one can invest poorly, how one is capable of gaining and losing interest in lovers without intending to do either, how some things retain their value because they are rare.   Having always spent Time like it was an arcade token, which is to say to spend it when we had it, this phone call is a vacation accrued after years of labor. The darkness stretches out in a room more familiar than the hotel room or a dorm room stripped bare, since this is my room, and you seem more familiar, more loved for your years of absence than when we lay absorbed by those rooms belonging to neither of us. You apologize for youth. I am awed and saddened by the difference in how we spent our twenties.

　　　Though I feel as if I have been given a great gift in your return, I will choose to pursue another lost love because the risk seems lower, more manageable given my emotionally impoverished state in this terrible town.   When I write to tell you this, you say it is as if you are standing on a dock, watching a boat pulling away; you see me wave from it, and you did not realize I was even on the boat. Though I will feel your cat eyes on me in the dark, I will rejoice in making a careful decision. The choice to love this other will later become a consolidation of all emotional losses and exceed them horribly, at the same time, but at this moment, I consider myself simply lucky to have secured access to your life again.

Overdrawn

You are 34, and I am 38. I look at Facebook for the third time this morning to see if you have responded to my comment about *Pina* in 3D. I consider adding Adrienne and Claire, your two best friends, and remind myself, again, that I have never and will never meet these women, though we speak through your wall to each other like Pyramus and Thisbe. We speak about you, around you, and you "like" everything we say. Two years ago, you consider visiting here but have no money; and I consider buying half your ticket. I consider going there myself, but I have vowed never to go to you again, or to listen to Tori Amos. I have moved back to Seattle to save what was left of me after Missouri and the break-up with the other one I loved, which caused me to sob until my top rib slips out of place to make room for the sadness. It has taken two years to recover. A friend, upon seeing your picture on my wall, says you look like my new boyfriend, and at times, she is right. He finds my spirit generous, and the love is true and supportive. You respond to one out of every five messages, and I send one more immediately, in which I ask you more questions than you will ever answer, beginning the wait again.

Armed Robbery

You are 36, and I am 40. I step off the plane in Austin, dressed in all white, and you step out of the car to pick me up. I said I would never go to Tulsa again, and I haven't, but I have forced my way here, instead, your new home of a week. It is a big moment, but I hate your hair. Your cat eyes are puffy from drinking again, and you tell me, as we get in the car, that if you act weird, it is because you took an Adderall yesterday to help you finish some work. We have two nice hours and a bottle of wine before you yell at me. I do not understand that it doesn't take much for drinkers to get angry because I do not understand addiction, my own drinking heavy but not daily or in secret. We are on your bed, listening to the CD I made you, just for this night, and I tell you if you yell at me again, I will leave. You apologize, as Beck's "Lost Cause" comes on. I think: if God exists, he manifests primarily as a DJ.

We canoe on the lake the next day and try to have all the conversations for which we never had time, try to make up for lost time. But the time is already lost—I could not make love last night after you yelled at me, could not sleep, and each time you touch me, I pull away, despite the years I have spent wanting just that. There is a new love back home in Seattle, but I tell him that this trip is one I have to make in order to be whole, one last heist before I quit for good. Before you are even awake that first morning, I call him, tell him that this trip is not going well, that this was a mistake, and that I love him, love him, love him. He tells me to get through the next two days and then come home to him. He will listen to the CD I made, until then.

I do not make it two days. The second night we drink heavily: I am desperate to have fun, having disliked you all day—your arrogance without accomplishment, your bitter rage at your 24-year-old ex-girlfriend, your mother, your son, your life, your need to smoke a cigarette or weed or take a pill or drink every two hours; you are angry at me in that way only lust can fuel and want to blur my edges, if you cannot have my soft body. We drink until we are drunk, and then we drink some more, get in your car, and suddenly the tumblers click, the safe is open, and the alarm inside of me goes off, as we speed down the highway and you begin to yell at me again. You are not my treasure, this has not been worth it, and I think that we might die, the car going faster, and I pray for the first time in years, really pray. You notice I am white-faced, that I refuse to look at you or talk. And so, you yell and yell, swerving to scare me more, laughing when you do. This is not my sweet-faced lover at 12, or, maybe, it always has been.

We arrive at the apartment, and I run upstairs, find my suitcase, start to pack. It is three in the morning. You push me on the bed and somehow there's a knife, but I am sobbing with my eyes closed, and a voice from my mouth stumbles as it repeats the thing even it cannot believe it says: please don't kill me please don't kill me. You let me up, I grab my bag and run from you, as I always knew I should, run from the scene of this crime against my heart and maybe yours, run in this strange neighborhood until I reach a Walgreen's, and the night manager takes me into the back room, gives me a bottle of water, wipes the blood that is, thank god, not my own off of my arm, and tells me, as I cry and hate myself, "Girl, we've all been there. You got away, and you never need to go back."

Safe Deposit Box

Y ou are 18, and I am 22. It is one in the morning, and the knock on the door startles me so that I feel sick. I open the door, and you are finally here. Your eyes are clear, and you are wearing a straw-colored tee shirt the color of your shoulder-length hair. In the sodium light, you are so golden, you are so beautiful, that it brings tears to my eyes. Here, in memory, I stay with you in that doorway forever, owing nothing to you or to myself but that which we owe to love, which never forgives a debt, and so we keep on paying until there's nothing, nothing left.

94

What Is the Light?

What is the light / that you have / shining all around you? / Is it chemically derived?
'Cause if it's natural / something glowing from inside / shining all around you / its
potential has arrived.

—*The Flaming Lips*

In the Beginning, There Was Light

I. *Radiation.*

Radius = ray as the root. To radiate: 1) to issue or emerge in rays, 2 to spread out or converge radically, as the spokes of a wheel or 3 to irradiate or illuminate (an object.)

Meanwhile, "radiant," the adjective, is "consisting of or emitted as radi-ation," to be "filled with happiness, joy or love," or to be "the apparent celestial origin of a meteoric shower."

Object and subject at once. To be that which engulfs a being in light and heat, and also to be engulfed—the "celestial origin" and the vessel.

I will begin radiation treatment next week: five days a week, for six weeks.

First Irony: I don't have cancer. My throat and mouth, possibly, will be burnt, as might my left cheek and neck, and there's a probability I will lose some of my hair. ("Your hair!" my friends exclaim, looking alarmed—I have beautiful hair. I will probably want mostly smooth foods, and I may lose my taste for alcohol. God forbid.

Second Irony: Although I don't have cancer, I will feel like I do, without, of course, the considerable weight of, perhaps, death pend-ing.

II. *How to Lose It All (or Most of It)*

In my late twenties, I had what's called a benign parotid tumor on my salivary gland. The doctor did a facelift incision behind my ear, left a scar, and gave me some Percocet. I healed, watching mostly Vietnamese movies (beautiful images, incomprehensible plots, drugged, for two or so weeks. At happy hours to come, friends would play games with my ear, testing nerve damage. "Does this hurt?" they'd say, pinching my ear. "Are you pinching yet? You can start pinching now." My ear would remain unresponsive, and they would test it further. "Let's hold the candle under her ear," said one. All in all, it wasn't a bad time.

In my mid-thirties, I noticed the scar above my ear becoming thicker. When I wore sunglasses, the scar hurt. "My scar hurts. I think Voldemort is near," I'd tell my sister. Four months later, my eyeglasses were chronically lopsided when I wore them at night. I took to lying on my side, to keep them in place as I read E. M. Forster novels about people oblivious to the growing dangers of their situations.

Consumed by teaching and distracted by impending university budget cuts, my mind, as they say, was elsewhere. So, it made sense that my hairdresser, Jordan, a woman whose primary goal is to make me look like Jessica Rabbit, would be the one to notice that this was no ordinary scar.

"Jesus! What is that?"

"My scar—you've seen it before."

"Noooo—it wasn't sticking out of your head like that. You need to check that out." I made the appointment the same week I was told the university budget cut meant, for our department, my job.

The first doctor said it was just scar tissue. She was also eight months pregnant and, I think I am generous in saying this, it seems her mind was also elsewhere. Eventually, I saw another doctor, who said it was a tumor, two and a half centimeters long. I then saw another doctor, who confirmed the tumor (for insurance purposes), adding, as he gently felt down the left side of my face, "Boy! You have all kinds of things going on there." In addition to my job, some other cuts would have to be made. On my face.

I ran into my department chair in a coffee shop, just minutes after the first CAT scan. I couldn't resist telling him. It was pure schadenfreude: he didn't want to lay me off. Still, I took pleasure, deep pleasure, within my increasingly self-pitying heart, that he, too, was shocked and horrified. Without my job, I'd lose my health insurance within a month after surgery. We're at a Jesuit school, devoted, they say, to social justice. It felt awful, awkward. Unreal. Not really pleasurable at all.

III. CAT Scan: You Are Not Your Body

You become a subway,
heading for the light

You are a warm towel
coming from the dryer

You are a block of deli cheese,
going through the slicer

You are a conduit for dye,
pumping to find darkness

You are both the fi re and the fl ame,
and you put your own self through it.

IV. At Least I Make This Cut

Two weeks prior to surgery day, at a party, I'd drunkenly told
a professor of European studies that I loved anesthesia because it was
"like death. It's awesome. So quiet, so comforting." This normally
doesn't work as a pick-up line, but he was German, so it did. After he
pulled me onto the basement stairs and kissed me, he proposed a book
project on the pleasures of anesthesia.

So, as I lie swaddled in hospital gown and blankets and those
little socks with non-skid tread on the bottom (perhaps one of the most
surprising forms of comfort, with the tube attaching to the needle in
my arm, I ask the anesthesiologists why they chose to go into anesthesia. Their answers are mundane (more money, less complicated than
surgery. I like better the reason my therapist posited: "They don't like
people, but they want to help. So, they help you by making the 'person'
part go away." This seems to hold true, since there's no ritual "count
backwards from ten"—the needle's been slipped in before I hit my third
question, and I am denied the pleasure of anticipating going under.
Seven hours later, my mother, sister and niece receive the news: they're
tumors!! Several more than we'd thought! Deeper! Hidden under my
salivary gland (which had to be taken out like almonds in a cake, curling
like vines around other tumors, seeding "like rows of glistening white
beads," Dr. Rowland says later—pearls along the strings of my facial
nerves. He's cut down the left side of my face, separating the trian-

gular piece of ear from the rest of my ear, then back and to the left, like the Kennedy assassination, onto my neck. I have a drain—a thick plastic tube—running underneath my face, from temple to neck, where it emerges like the wellhead on some bizarre oil well. This tube ends in a plastic sack, which collects the draining blood. This, I call, for the entertainment of my *Twilight*-obsessed niece, a blood canteen. "You're a snack!" she squeals, as she empties it periodically, since my sister and mother are not up to the task. (In ten years, she is an ER nurse, compassionate and laughing as she cares for your body.

In my favorite picture from that time, I'm holding the blood canteen up with one hand, away from my chest, and smiling, as if it were a gold medallion, but I don't yet feel like a winner of anything.

V. MRI: *Must Read Interpretatively*

One Tuesday, months before, I spent most of the day with my friend Chris, a notorious commitment-phobe, at his house. We had tea, talked about my job loss, his impending career transition, and made plans for his birthday party that Saturday. I asked him if he was still dating Sara, the girl he'd met at my housewarming in August. "Yeah," said he. "It's going pretty well. So, I'm making French 75's at the bar later . . . . ." On his birthday, then, when I saw said Sara, I congratulated her on the truly remarkable feat of getting Chris to continue to date her for more than a month.

Sara (beaming): Yeah! We moved in together!

Me (stunned and instantly suspicious): When?

Sara (innocent and still beaming): Tuesday!

Later, when Chris stumbles past me, I catch him by the hand not holding a drink.

"You moved IN with her??" I hiss.

"I was going to tell you when I had more time alone with you," he whispers, clearly panicked.

"Why didn't you tell me Tuesday, then, when we were alone, like, ALL DAY?"

Glancing quickly to make sure Sara is still cutting his birthday cake (which, I might add, she has made and decorated all by herself), Chris rolls his eyes. "I kept thinking if I just didn't talk about it, I could keep denying it was going to happen."

That's how I feel about radiation.

Yet I feel as if I should write about it. "You're unemployed!" my friends (with jobs) rejoice. "You can just write and take care of yourself! You will become famous. You will be like Frida Kahlo. You will write the story of your pain and make it beautiful." While the thought of my own bio-pic appeals to me, I am still struggling to get over the loss of my job—a job for which I'd quit my higher-paying, more secure tenure-track job, just so I could return to Seattle and not waste away in Missouri. A Ph. D. in loving words doesn't seem to be doing much for me, in terms of security. And they want me to spend my summer writing? Depression may make for good material, but you have to be able to bring yourself to do anything with that material.

I think denial is better suited to a blank page.

June

So far, my summer includes three visits to the doctor a week, as they use the CAT scan, and now an MRI, to make a grid of my face, to pinpoint exactly where the spokes of radiation will stream towards the centerpiece of my cheek. Not only am I on unemployment for the fi rst time in my life, I begin paying for health insurance next month, with the help of Obama. Man, that guy is Jesus with a budget. I am the poster girl for the Obama Socialist Agenda.

The MRI is funny. They put you in a Storm Trooper hel-met, cover you with a blanket, and slip you into a tube. You feel like a Twinkie: packaged and shelved. Then the sounds start, changing constantly in key and frequency, sounding the waters of my face for unknown objects: the hulls of cancerous cell ships, a piece of tumor fl otsam. "The scans will last 18 minutes total," someone says, from another room, over a microphone. "This fi rst one will last four seconds . . . this one 16 . . . this one will last ten minutes." Each with a different sound: submarine, dial-up internet connecting, D fl at followed by the sound of laundry drying. I am being mapped. I am Tron.

VI. Making the Mask: Becoming a Storm Trooper

When someone loses a job they love and undergo surgery, words like "tumor" and sentences such as "damage to the facial nerve is possible" fl oat like ashes through what's left of your resolve. If you see this happening to a friend, if you would, do please avoid saying these two very dumb things:

1.	Everything happens for a reason.
2.	You're strong / brave / courageous / staying
positive. Good for you!

Concerning #1: Setting aside the more complex existential issues surrounding this notion, there are so many things about this that irritate me. I moved back to Seattle when I realized that my integrity was suffering in my tenure-track job in Missouri. Though I loved my colleagues and several students, education wasn't really a priority: "D means Degree" was a popular slogan amidst the students. I was the only single woman within miles who wasn't a local, a divorced local or an alcoholic (yet), and I knew not many professors who really wanted to be there. We *did* enjoy each other and held dinners, parties, and space for each other. Truly, Missouri loves company.

Yet, existentialist issues considered, this was too much struggle—struggle that perhaps, would lead me to greater liberty but which seemed to be leading to the death of my soul. I'd never been one to follow a "plan" or to do what others tell me, but the path promised by the PhD seemed authentic: to lead to the kind of life I could want. It should not have been surprising to find that my perception of my self-worth, over seven years, had become far more intertwined with the tenure-track plan than I'd thought. The difficulty of letting go of that plan surprised me. But I had to—no number of Dickens novels distracted me from my own misery. The severity of this became clear when, sitting on my couch, in the midst of a blizzard, I found myself saying out loud, "Who am I *doing* this for?" Or it could have been the time I found myself wondering how much it would really hurt to hang myself. One morning, I slipped on the steep stairs from my upstairs bedroom and fell down the entire flight, smashing my coffee cup against the wall as I went and cutting my hand on the ceramic shards. Lying in a pool of blood and coffee, I burst into tears, exclaiming with only the startled cat to hear, "I *hate* living alone." The cat ran away, and I crawled to the couch to cry until I could comfort myself.

Moving back to Seattle was the first massive life choice I'd made based purely on what *I* wanted to do—rather than on what should happen next on this path to adulthood. What "reason" might, then, onslaughts of tumors illuminate? My choice was not impulsive or ill-considered. I refuse to believe the tumors were indicative that any decision fueled by integrity needs a brutal corrective. If there was a reason for losing my job and growing a crop of tumors in my face, I can only imagine it might have been this: "It would have been worse in Missouri. If you'd died there, no one would have found you for days, and your cat would have eaten your nose."

Secondly, I might accept that everything does, in fact, happen for a reason, if only I learned the reasons for things one at a time. Instead, however, everything happens at once and piles on top of everything else, like dirty laundry when you're out of quarters. Sure—you may get one load done here or there, but inevitably, the black vee-neck you need is still in the bottom of the hamper. By the time you get to it, you don't need long sleeves. Hindsight, like a clean black vee-neck, often comes after the need for it is over.

Concerning #2: This is a degradation of the word "brave." "Brave" is breaking up with someone you really love, knowing that if you stayed together, you could be content, but instead, you face the scarier possibility that you might be happier alone. "Brave" is stopping a fight on the street by stepping in, instead of running across the street to call for help, or blowing the whistle on the Mafia, instead of accepting the offer you were told you couldn't refuse. In short, "brave" is doing something you know to be right when you have the option not to do it.

Having tumors isn't about "right" or "choice." As my current prognosis implies, what with its "probabilities" of hair loss and "possible" burnt throats, it's all about chance. There's nothing I did to incite the cellular riot in my tissues; there's no carcinogenic I could have avoided to keep my skin beautiful and unmarked. Needing a reason for everything denies possibility, particularly the possibility that even our bodies, maybe our souls, are on a roulette wheel with too much staked on red 21. Even Jesus had his moment in the garden of Gethsemane: "Lord, if it is possible, let this cup be taken from me." And even if I don't believe in him, I believe in the notion that it is brave to die when you have a choice not to. Getting radiation so that small children won't stare at you and men might still want to date you . . . I don't think we should give out many prizes for that.

I did ask my doctor what a cowardly patient would act like— how "non-bravery" would look. He laughed and said that they would put off treatment and fall prey to more anxiety . . . but I think he basically agreed with my reasoning: you must do it, and you can cry about it, but you're not brave, sister.

I will admit that the making of the mask does make me cry and that anyone reading this should feel very, very sorry for me. The mask is this plasticine mesh—it looks like that in which they wrap Asian pears; they wet it with warm water and press it all over your head, face, neck and shoulders until it hardens completely. Jurgen, the kindly Eastern European who is solely in charge of this process, jokes that this is the part of radiation that is the "Group Health spa." The mask hardens, enabling the doctors to plot which of those tiny little holes in the mesh will be the portals for pinpointed radiation—kind of like city planners deciding where the streetlights should go on the grid of my facial metropolis.

So far, so good. But wait! They also *bolt down* the mask, all around your upper half, so it hardens as close to your face as possible. So close that if you swallow, it's uncomfortable because it changes the shape of that weird, gradual hardening. It's so close you can't open your eyelids or lips, though there's a hole for your nose . . . but that's it. If you were to try to raise your head, even to lift your shoulders, you would, I assure you, completely and totally freak out. Imagine it now. Imagine it again, but worse.

The first time I do it, my breath comes in little gasps, little terrors. I tell myself, again and again, "Stop it. Stop it. Stop it. Stop it."

And I will be bolted down into this shape five days a week, for six weeks. My job will be paralysis, pretending to be a plaster cast. This first time, I just focus on breathing—modified yoga since deep breathing is also uncomfortable. I breathe and try to think of songs that aren't too bouncy, so I won't want to move my head.

And so, in lieu of music, my mind turns exactly to that I don't want to think about: to another loss I've been trying to breathe out of my system for the past year.

❧

Two summers ago, I am so happy that I find myself frustrated I'm unable to verbalize how happy I am. I almost believe that, even if there is no God, there might well be a reason for some things because I feel so lucky so #blessed and so right to be with Sam—my friend of eleven years, my always-soul mate, recently divorced and finally mine[3]. Mine, to love and laugh with and . . . . recently divorced. Mine to punch in front of the Jefferson Memorial, when he tries to justify cheating on me by saying he thinks I am "desperate" to get married. I think of this as I lie, all by myself, on this table. A Persian Jew, whose marriage fell apart,

---
[3] See "Divorce Closet."

in part, because his wife felt smothered by culture, religion, and his dominating father, Sam is a 37-year-old man whose fondness for Disney's *Peter Pan* is telling. There is no way he could ever do this alone—nor would he be allowed to even try it. His whole family would insist upon inspecting the mesh and personally pressing it onto his, admittedly, lovely face.

I stop speaking to him in June, after figuring out he'd cancelled our Memorial Weekend trip to be with another woman. In August, he starts calling . . . by which time I've moved back to Seattle without telling him. And though the first words he speaks to me in September are "I can't live without you—I'm obsessed," he is also still dating the other woman. But, he swears, he has been grieving me the whole time. What kind of woman puts up with a man actively grieving another woman in front of her?

Oh wait. A woman like *me*.

Still, I listen when he starts sending me the CDs—six, total, which he made during August—and they all agree: he can't live without me. But I am going to have to live without him.

I won't even bother to detail the miniscule negotiations and additional injuries that ensue. (Did I really have to clarify that he *did* need to stop dating the other woman? Really?) They go on for months. The final blow comes when I text him in February about my impending biopsy. And I hear this: "Bryn, our romantic relationship is over. You can't expect that kind of support from me anymore. But I'm here for you as a friend."

Why, then, do I get the one in May from a Cure concert at Coachella: "They're playing 'Pictures of You'—let's rewrite the song"?

But I wasn't writing—or rewriting back anymore.

It's July now. I'm breathing, I'm thinking of this all, and as I lie here, I know he would cry if he saw me. That as I am losing my hair, which I am, in chunks—my beautiful hair—if he still loved me, he would pull me close and kiss my head and tell me I was beautiful anyway. I know that, if faced directly with me, bolted to a table and becoming the object, not the subject of the radiance he once knew, he would know, better than anyone I've ever known, how I would feel and what I would want to hear. In that moment. But because he has never done anything by himself, never given himself up to pure chance without secretly following a conventional plan, he is not here.

And the irony of this intertwining of chance and failed plans is what I think of as I lie on the table, holding a foam ring in my hands, to keep my arms close to my sides. And when they take off the mask, finally, I sit up and find that, whether it is because of him or because my eyelids are finally free to open, I am crying.

VII. The First Full Week: The Young Lover's Radiation Mix

I asked my friends to make me radiation mixes, so I can lie on the table and listen to something other than the intermittent "eeeeeeee" of radiation, of science entering my face. This week, radiation started on Tuesday, and my standing appointment was set for 3:30 every day, for the next six weeks, with weekends off. I'm introduced to three women, but Daphne's my favorite—in part because she's the beautiful one and in part because she's the only one I end up seeing every day. She loves my ring, and I silently vow to dress up for Daphne every day, since I have no students or colleagues to look nice for. They explain what will happen each day and what I can expect, yet I still feel unable to answer when people ask me how the mask prevents the radiation from going every-where. It seems to have something to do with vectors.

Day One

I decide to start with The Young Lover's cd. I know I have many friends thinking of me and my family loves me, but there is really no replacement for a lover because they are yours and yours alone, in some way. The Young Lover is 23, a recent sculpture graduate who'd been notoriously crushed out on me while I was a professor in Missouri. It was a crush I knew about, he had never been my student, and after I resigned, it didn't seem a rebound summer fling would kill anyone. And we were so happy, had so much fun. The Young Lover is not Sam, but he is still a constant joy, coming to visit me several times so far, staying for a whole month in January, just after his college graduation. He's not even really mine—he's not going to move here, there's clearly the obsta-cle of age, and I think he should be dating others. But he's the person to whom I can say "I love you" and who says it back to me.

The first song on his is an instrumental: "Ready Set Glow" by Atlas Sound. They put the cd on first, and I can barely hear it as they begin to put the mask on me. Oh god—the mask. I'd forgotten what it feels like, even though I knew I would have it on every day for this, but as they lay it over my face, I begin to panic a little. I close my eyes and breathe, focusing on how much the instrumental playing makes it seem

104

like a movie. They bolt it down, then take it off again, to make a little more room for my nose. Daphne tells me they're ready and that they'll turn up the music.

The door closes. The first song ends, and I hear little staccato piano chords: one two three four major four chords minor four chords. A sweet male voice starts singing and through my closed eyelids, I can see blue-violet light sweep across the left side of my face, a shadow on water. The radiation noise can't compete with this pretty song—it is Grizzly Bear's "Two Weeks"—and I feel so close to The Young Lover; it embodies all the sweetness and after-school specialness of his love for me. "I told you I would stay," this voice sings, and I know he would, if moving for a girl wasn't such a clichéd thing to do.

> *Would you always Maybe*
> *sometimes Make it easy*
> *Take your time*
>
> *Think of all the ways*
> *Momentary phase Just like*
> *yesterday*
> *I told you I would stay*

The chorus is so him. He really doesn't know what to do for me when I'm down or hurt or ill. "Oh," he mutters, unable to think of anything else when I'm crying, "Don't feel bad." The half-phrases echo all The Young Lover's half-articulated sentiments so well—while they don't really say anything, they indicate how hard our relationship has been for him to process, in terms of what comes next. And while they don't really get anywhere, they are beautiful to hear, as I lie here on this table, with no one to pick me up afterwards.

Day Two

Day Two has the vague sensation of already being routine, and the women tell me they like my music best of all patients ever. "Track fi ve is what we were up to, right?" one says. "Man, we love your music! Massive Attack? That's great. Most people bring in oldies." I wonder if this is because I am younger than most getting radiation. But that can't be true. Everyone gets cancer now.

Day Three

It's Thursday when I realize that I really, truly have to do this every day, for six more weeks, and that I hate it.

I hate it I hate it hate hate hate hate it. The mask presses so tightly into my forehead and my eyelids that it hurts, and I know that I will look corrugated after treatment for at least an hour. We're up to "Lionesse" by White Rabbits, but I forget to listen because I hate having the mask on so much. I hate it. I hate it. Yesterday's treatment felt like ten minutes; today's seems like a full hour. Jurgen, the sweet Eastern European guy who made my mask, is here today, and as they remove the mask and pull me up by my arms, I tell him, "The mask hurt today." He chuckles slightly, but sympathetically. "Yes but imagine if we'd had you wear the mouth guard. It would really be tight then—and we do want it to be tight." I know he's trying to get me to look on the bright side. If I'd had to wear the mouth guard, I would have choked on my saliva or died on the table from lack of air. Still, I feel mildly chastised. What I really want him to say is "I'm sorry. I am so sorry, Bryn."

This isn't even the end of the first week. This is not going to be quick. I cry all the way home.

Day Four: End of Week One

The drive to the hospital is, ironically, the same route I used to drive to work, and it takes about 20 minutes. Around minute eight, I find myself dreading today's treatment. It's because of Thursday. I know it. It's like when you realize you're going to have to break up with someone, but you don't feel like the timing's right. So, you keep driving to their house and watching movies, going out to dinner and feeling like a fraud because you know that you don't love them anymore, or that you love them terribly but you're not going to work out because you've now had this sneaky thought that you could do better or that you two will not be able to talk about anything but your children, if you stay together and grow old. With this relationship, me and radiation, that thought occurred on the second date of what will be a two-year relationship.

We don't quite finish The Young Lover's cd today—there's one track remaining—but I take it home, telling the Rad Girls I'll bring in a new one next week. The final track cracks me up a little; it's Enya, "Only Time." I didn't know TYL even knew who Enya was, much less that he would have any. I mean, I loved Enya in high school, but this song is truly the Pepsi commercial song. Or the Rolex commercial. I know it's a not-so-veiled reference to what he always tells me, when I ask him

106

to move out here: "We'll see. Not right now." But maybe also it's a way to think about these days of unemployment and doctor's appointments. Daphne and Other Woman sit me up, and I shake my head a little bit. "Your hair looks *great*," Other Woman says. Now I really laugh. "Thanks," I say, "It's my 'just-got-out-of-radiation look.'" And then I grow somber, wonder if she's wondering when I'm going to start losing it.

VII. Week Two: Gretchen's Mix

The camera broke today—the one through which they watch me. They watch to see if I freak out. If I start waving my hands, they know that something's wrong: that I'm going to throw up or that I'm scared. If anything, I wave my hands to signal when to skip a track. Being pinned down to listen to music over which I have no control is an excellent exercise in discipline, though I really haven't been tested. After all, these are my friends' mixes, and my friends are great. What I find is not that I dislike some songs but that I get bored with them. Frankly, I am coming to see radiation treatments as much-needed antidotes to the Pandora culture, which means we don't have to endure anything less than 100 percent to our taste, at any given moment. I wish I could do the same with my students and literature. "I'm going to bolt you down," I'd say, opening Matthew Arnold or Tennyson, "and I want you to just LISTEN and THINK about this."

Since this is Gretchen's mix, it's both funny and folksy, with one track entitled "She Left Me for Jesus." The Rad Girls, Daphne and Shelley, think this is hilarious. Gretch also puts "Eye of the Tiger" on as Track One. I request that they skip it—I mean, clearly it was just to make me laugh, and I do, but I will also want to laugh under the mask, which is, frankly, impossible and, even if it was possible, counter-productive. When I come in the next day, however, I find they still put the song to good use: Jurgen, the guy who made my mask, just did half an Iron Man in Eastern Washington (Iron Man from the Iron Curtain!, and the girls set up the cd player in the lounge so that when he came out of the changing room in his bike gear, the song started up. They said he rolled his eyes at them, giggling in the corner, but then began prancing down the hall for them, pumping his arms in the air. I love him.

New Observations:

*I was nauseated every day this week. Friday marked the end of nachos for a while since I threw them up that night.

*I finally figured out the sound the radiation rays make. It's the sound of an apartment buzzer, ringing incessantly for someone who's not ever going to be home again.

*When I see, through my luminescent eyelids, violet light passes over my eyes, I know we're almost down. I also know that I need to breathe in for three seconds and out for three, pushing the air out my mouth, so I can keep the hot spoon flavor of radiation out.

*The inside of the mask is starting to get glitter and lipstick on it. It's also slightly poky, like grass. Dry grass.

VIII. Week Three: Brandi's Mix and Becca's Mix

Highlights of the mixes: Both girls put on "Sneakin' Out of the Hospital" by the Beastie Boys. The irony of this is that it's just out that MCA, of said Boys, has been diagnosed with the cancerous version of THE SAME THING I HAVE. Same side of the face and everything. Guess we'll both be cancelling on Lollapalooza this year.

The routine of it all is starting to set in, so I'm starting to focus less on myself and my experience and more on the surroundings and the staff. The front desk women and I compliment each other's clothes every day, and I noticed Jurgen had a tan, which is how I found out about the Half Iron Man. Daphne is beautiful—a true Capitol Hill hipster, with black-framed funky glasses, black hair with red streaks and my taste in jewelry and music. Every day, they all compliment me on my jewelry or my dress and say, "OOOO—Daphne! That is SO you! She's your sister!!" I love that because Daphne is so beautiful. She looks beautiful in dark purple scrubs. Shelley seems like a misplaced PR woman—she wears heels and dresses. I wonder what's up with that. Carol is the talker of the three—she's a former Iowan. I totally called it—the commitment to Seattle, to hip music, yet the strange knowledge of sports and how to be constantly friendly to strangers. They're almost all autumn birthdays—I start the set:

October: Bryn
November : Carol
December: Shelley
May: Daphne

Or Daphne starts us. Oh life. Your circles.

There's some other sweet blonde woman—I can't tell if she's part of their crew or just learning. She's the one who noticed my "great" hair, that I am a radioactive Charlie's Angel.

I interview them all, informally. Here's what they say:

Do you like your jobs?
We love our jobs. We love them. This department is so much better than the MRI department.
Why?
They're tense. We're a family.

What's a bad patient like? If a patient's difficult, how's that manifest?

A lot of patients are angry with us—they resent us. We know it's not us. They got a late diagnosis or they don't understand why this has to happen to them.

What are the most desirable qualities in a radiology tech?
Anal retentive. Perfectionist.
The kind of person who'll straighten a picture frame?
Exactly.
Did you ever want to do another kind of job?
Daphne was a social worker. (I knew it! She likes clothes too much to have always been in the medical field—most nurses seem to go for bling over vintage, and most hospital staff seem to favor sportswear.)
What makes you terrified for a patient? What's the worst thing that can happen?

Oh . . . Not getting there in time to get the mask off. Patients with throat cancer . . . they get nauseous and. . . .

They throw up in the mask??
Yeah. That just happened the other day. It's terrible . . . they can be asphyxiated.

∞

Welcome to my new greatest fear: vomiting, bolted down in that mask. I would FREAK OUT. Jesus.

Ann!! My beloved best friend Ann is here ALL week! Just for me! Leaving her two children and precious husband! And Minneapolis! For me!

Best friends are the best.

Perfect timing: they were right about the first few weeks. That was just a matter of yoga breathing and rethinking my time. I can tell this is week four because suddenly, I am exhausted. I take naps in the middle of the day. I drink water constantly because I'm always thirsty, and even though I force myself to go out for sushi with Annie twice, I don't feel like eating. Nothing tastes good, or, for that matter, smells good; and so, nothing sounds good. I take the trash out the minute there's anything in it. The citrus scented Swiffers nearly make me barf. I can't eat bread or chips because I don't have enough saliva, so anything with flour in it turns me into Dog Eating Peanut Butter. I get halfway through a bagel and have to choke it out in the bushes beside the front porch. Later, my neighbor mentions he can't understand why his chihuahua always wants to investigate back there. I know why. I've had to spit food out before.

Not eating, not drinking alcohol . . . okay. I'm getting skinny. Americans eat too much, anyway. I've never been a fruit person, and suddenly, I'm in love with all these luscious orchard fruits—probably because they're juicy / palatable for Dog Eating Peanut Butter mouth. I eat plums and BLUEBERRIES. God! I've never UNDERSTOOD the blueberry! It's beautiful—the kind of blue you hope to see in the eyes of some smoldering, black-haired Heathcliffian figure . . . . They're little, you can eat them compulsively, they're not sticky, it seems there was a bumper crop . . . . Oh, blueberries. Yum.

But . . . .

My hair is falling out. Last Friday, I brushed my hair, and a giant clump came out. It was just like you hear. I brushed it again, and another came out. I stopped brushing.

Ann notices it first. Getting ready to go out one night, I put my hair in two doggy ears. My back is to Ann, and I hear her intake of breath. "Oh . . . honey. You . . . can't wear your hair like that." I feel, and while the bald spots were previously limited to the left side, behind my ear, under my hair, there's now a spot (a "contra," Dr. Rowland says) on the other side—a kind of exit wound from the radiation. It's true that my hair is long enough to cover all these newly barren places, but that's not the point. I don't CARE that no one notices. I notice now that my beautiful, thick hair, which I can usually put in a bun with no pins, just tucking my own hair into a tight knot, is not thick. It's anemic. It looks straggly. It looks like I should be in a TV movie about an overworked, heroin-addict mom, who just got fired from her check-out counter job. The blonde girl at radiation doesn't say my hair looks great anymore. My friend Carly asks if I got a haircut, and I said, "No. It's falling out. Actually, it's layered—the long layers are on the top, and on the bottom—nothing." I think of Jo, from *Little Women*, and Amy's exclamation when she sees that Jo has cut off her hair to sell: "Oh Jo! Your one true beauty!"

Every time I brush it, while Ann is here, I take out what's on the brush and put it in the bottom drawer. We're going to make Victorian hair jewelry out of it . . . if only we can find a book on how to do it. "I tried to find one, but it seems to have gone out of fashion," Ann says. We laugh hysterically.

Despite Ann's reassurance that you can't even tell, I hate it so much. And I will kill the next person who says, "It's just hair—it'll grow back." I will kill them like "Porphyria's Lover" kills her in the Browning poem—I will take a strand of my own remaining hair and wind it around their necks until the strand breaks or they do.

The bald spots are like no feeling I've ever known on my own head, but I know exactly what they feel like. They feel like a very bald baby's head. This is what, once, my baby head felt like.

Ann mops my floor, makes me stop playing and come in for naps. We laugh and read *The Ex-Boyfriend Cookbook* out loud. We shop. And when I take her to the airport on Friday, I come home and sleep for three and a half hours. I get up, brush my teeth, and go back to bed.

Elena's mix ends with the Presidents of the United States' classic: "Lump."

She's lump / she's lump / she's lump / she's in my head She's lump / she's lump / she's lump / she might be dead

Week Five: Leo's Mix, The Gay Upstairs Neighbor's Mix, and Two Ac-cidental Norah Jones Songs.

Fuck, I'm tired.
Tired, tired, tired. Really tired. SO tired. "Awake" seems like an imposition.

Fortunately, the weather continues to be . . . NOT summer.

Rainy, cold. I don't ever look cute anymore—at least, I don't try to. I've worn jeans every day this week—the clearest sign I'm not feeling well.

This week is surreal. I'm basically sleeping until noon, getting up, checking email, drinking a cup of coffee (out of habit—not because it tastes good), eating some plums and going to radiation around 3. Coming home around 4:15, getting back into bed. I've read at least three books this week. I don't even think anymore. I'm just surviving this last full week—found out I don't have to do SIX full weeks—just Monday of next week, and then I'm done.

This is good because the left side of my face is totally scorched now. It annoys me when people pretend not to notice it. Come on. If you don't notice it, then you make me feel crazy, as well as sick. My skin's almost grey—it's really just severe sunburn, just past the point of tan. My ear is sore, and my throat feels crispy inside. I'm always thirsty. Always. And I wake up every day with a very thickly coated tongue. I think of that Bugs Bunny cartoon, in which he goes to the doctor, says his tongue is coated, sticks out his tongue, and it's wearing a little white coat, buttoned up to the top. I literally scrape off my lips with my fingernail.

Sexy, no? I went on a one-hour date on Monday, too. I met this guy, Peter, at a birthday party the week before Ann came, two weeks ago, when I still felt human. We'd talked about the Beatles, and he'd kissed me goodnight. The kiss had been good, and I like the Beatles, so I gave him my number. When he asked when we could get together, I suddenly realized what that would entail: energy. Even if we just went out for coffee, I'd be with someone who didn't know me well . . . which made me wonder who I am right now. Sleepy. Shorter tempered. Forgetful, less talkative, thin-haired, burnt skinned, less fun.

I told him that since I went to bed around 4:30 and couldn't really eat anything, it seemed an afternoon coffee for one hour before radiation was about the only first date option.

It was ok. He walked me to the hospital—it was across the street. The radiology girls thought that was hilarious.

Peter called me yesterday, but seriously. I can barely get out of bed, much less really care about pursuing a relationship that, so far, doesn't seem particularly "there." Could we just skip to the part where we're six months in, we've had sex, he's seen me sick before and can just lie in bed and watch movies with me? I'd go ahead and ask, but he does something with business for a living, blah blah working. I'm tempted to stick to my gay upstairs neighbor.

"Gay upstairs neighbor or dorky boy who has a crush on me?" "Dorky boy who has a crush on you!" So, we start Leo's CD. The girls vote it off the island after just one session. Sorry, Leo. You obviously didn't think about what Sonic Youth would sound like, bolted to a table. We move on to GUN's (Gay Upstairs Neighbor's).

But, as I'm bolted into the mask (at which point I usually stop speaking), and Nicole (new team member) presses play, I hear . . . not Crystal Castles or The Knife or any of GUN's other fabulous selections . . . but what sounds suspiciously like . . . Norah Jones. I wave my arms, a little frantically. "Mmmrrph!" I am trying to say "This isn't his!!!" I hope that was clear. I try again, my lips just barely able to move against the itchy mask's screen: "The Gay Upstairs Neighbor doesn't listen to Norah Jones! I don't listen to Norah Jones!" "But isn't his cd 'Electric Lady Land'?" asks sweet Nicole. "MMM," I agree, "but . . . ." "Well, let's try track two," she murmurs, trying to soothe me. Norah again! There's a pause, and I think they've left the room, left me to Norah Jones. I sigh and tell myself, internally, to grow up. There are worse things than being bolted to a table, listening to Norah Jones and being radiated. I could throw up in the mask. There's always that—instant silver lining to anything.

But Nicole comes through for me: "Oh, silly me! I've put two CDs in at once! Norah was on bottom!"

Norah, incidentally, belongs to Jurgen. *That* is funny.

~~~

Daphne says goodbye forever on Thursday. I wasn't ready for this. She hugs me twice and says she hopes she doesn't have to see me there again. I don't deal with this very well. I go home and stay in bed. Monday seems like it will be so monumental, but I can't think of what it will be like.

It's like losing a job again.

Epilogue: Last Week and Recovery

They hear me coming down the hall and chirp, "Last day! Last Day!" I tell them my birth date for the twenty-sixth time and tell them I expect a card. I walk past the monitors and around the corner to the table. "Surprise!" They've made me a certificate, admitting me to the "Favorite Patient Club." I'm sure they give it to everyone, but I am touched and tear up a bit. The certificate rewards me for being "cheerful, courageous, tolerant, and determined." Hey! I AM all of those things . . . except for "determined." Three out of four. Determined?

Determined to do . . . what? "Tolerant" really covers anything I could imagine, regarding the actual endurance of it all.

Having the weekend off always makes me notice how much better I feel when I have even two days off. Amazing. We do so much to our bodies, and they just bounce back . . . or start to explore bouncing back. There's much hugging when this final time is over, and I promise them all a compilation of the radiation mixes. It takes me a few weeks to feel like making it, but I do it.

And here's the playlist—song title, band, and maker:

Ready Set Glow: The Best of Bryn's Radiation Mixes
*Electricity (The Avalanches) *Brandi*
*Power's On (The Go! Team) *Becca*
*Two Weeks (Grizzly Bear) *The Young Lover*
*Lump (Presidents of USA) *Elena*
*Radar (Britney Spears) *Gay Upstairs Neighbor*
*Eye of the Tiger (Survivor) *Gretchen*
*Sneaking Out of the Hospital (Beastie Boys) *Becca & Brandi*
*The Conductor (The Faint) *GUN*
*Atoms for Peace (Thom Yorke) *Brandi*
*Fried My Little Brains (The Kills) *Brandi*
*Our Life Is Not a Movie or Maybe (Okkervil River) *Gretchen*
*The Queen's Corner (Joel Alme) *Leo*
*She Left Me for Jesus (Hayes Carll) *Gretchen*
*Some Things You Never Get Used To (The Supremes) *Becca*
*Vanished (Crystal Castles) *GUN*
*Save Ginny Weasley (Harry & the Potters) *Becca*
*'Til My Head Falls Off (They Might Be Giants) *Becca*
*Sunlight Makes me Paranoid (Elefant) *GUN*
*Right in the Head (M. Ward) *Becca*
*Dancin' in the Dark (the Ding! String Trio) *Becca*
*Neighborhood #3—Power Out (Arcade Fire) *Brandi*

I choose in terms of the most soothing, while bolted down. "Two Weeks" still wins, though the staff favorite is still "She Left Me for Jesus." Funniest? "Save Ginny Weasley" and "Some Things You Never Get Used To." Becca's overall CD was funniest; Brandi's and GUN's win for total album delight, though this irritates Leo, who considers himself a mix tape expert, to no end. Dude, it wasn't a contest. Even though I'm giving out firsts.

I go to see Amy, the LPN, one last time, and I've lost 15 pounds. Rah. Easy enough, when all one can eat are plums. She winces a little when she sees my neck. "Does it burn a little to put the aloe on now?" "Yes." I've blistered near my collarbone. Um, weren't all the tumors in my CHEEK? Why'd I get burned down there?

She gives me something called Aquaphor, which rivals Abreva, I tell Gretchen, for "Jesus in a Tube." It's greasy, so I give up on trying to make my hair (what's left of it) cute and pull it into a ballet mistress bun every day, giving the burn wide range to heal. Tuesday, I see some old work friends, which gives me the chance to see how someone other than Gay Upstairs Neighbor reacts to my neck. The girls look concerned and then, the flurry of reassurance begins: "OH, no, it doesn't look that bad not what I expected very quick healing I'm sure." I see them a week later, and their collective sigh of relief is palpable and a little funny. "OH god, that's SO much better."

I'll say—it's not blistering anymore. Yay, Aquaphor!!

I'm satisfied with so little now. Useful, really.
OH WAIT! Now I have to start worrying about my future again. Sigh.

I tell Jill, my therapist, how disappointed in myself I am that my whole summer is over and I haven't made any interesting progress, in terms of getting my life together. She looks at me, mouth open. "You just finished radiation. You are tired. You had big, big things happen this summer, and you got two classes at North. Be kind to yourself! You are recovering. Do I really have to tell you this?" For some reason, I start sobbing. "It's just . . . I feel . . . it's . . . now that radiation's over, I feel depressed again because I don't . . and winter's coming, and I don't want to crash again, I just can't . . . ." Poor Jill gives me that "Oh Honey" look. "Oh honey," she says, sympathetically. "You're just tired, ok? And you're not going to crash again."

I feel a little better now.

But I want to see Sam again. Is it just because it's August, and that's when he tried to come back last year? Is it because I want him to see my neck and hair and feel sorry for me? It's not really because I'm ready to be friends again. I think it's because I'm tired, and that means I'm too tired to be angry. I just want to talk face to face—too much emailing and too much time on the phone, and this major thing consumed seven months of my life. I just want him to recognize that. Then what? I am so weirdly vindictive with ex-boyfriends—I think I'm not, but if a chance to guilt them comes up, I'll take it, with cream. Where's that come from?

I'm just tired.

Once again, I face the end of a summer with what I hope will be some new face or new trick for happiness. Last year, it was to remember that nothing has to be permanent—that you can just pack up the truck and the cat and drive back to Seattle. This year, it might be that most things can be dealt with, if you know there's an end in sight. Maybe that's why I want to see Sam again—so I can see if there's an end in sight, a real end, not just abandonment. But I've also spent the summer listening to indie music, and on Gretchen's cd, Okkervil River says, *This is a life story / so there's no climax.*

I just really, really want to be happy for an extended stretch of time—let's say, two years. Happy in a long, boring but fulfilling way, without these huge emotional or financial or intellectual turnovers. Just some time well-spent in this healed body, with that certainty that I'm doing enough and doing what I can, with the promise and likelihood that the happiness of one day is a preview of the happiness tomor-row. I don't want anymore "life lessons" and I don't want to be tested or "made stronger." I want the time and the space to appreciate what I do know, and I want to be able to believe that I might not be doing that badly at all.

Playlist Three

Just Burning: Songs of Joy, Divided

OMD
> *"Sailing on the Seven Seas"* and *"Souvenir"*

Devo
> *"Time Out for Fun"* and *"Whip It"*

The Beatles
> *"Something"*

Eric Clapton
> *"Layla"*

Animal Collective
> *"Did You See the Words Today"*

Otis Redding
> *"These Arms of Mine"*

Kate Wolf
> *"Cornflower Blue"*

Nikka Costa
> *"Everybody Got Their Something"*

High School Orchestral Maneuvers in the Dark
and in Broad Daylight

Today is high school graduation in my tiny Kansan hometown. My niece, Allison, has 20-some people in her class; I graduated from the same high school with 38 in mine. It's 97 degrees, windy, and the weather forecast is for hail and possible tornadoes. Upstairs, my sister Amber is frantically putting Pepto-Bismol pink plastic tablecloths over several card tables, battling the wind, and Allie already told me not to expect much from the choir's rendition of "Sweet Caroline."

I'm trying to remember my own graduation. I know that Dena[4] and I were bummed that I missed being Salutatorian by a few points because we didn't get to give our speeches together, although I helped co-write the speech anyway. (It included the phrase "Although our class had as much in common as Peter Pan and Satan.") I know that I had Pat Miller cake afterwards; my brother-in-law's mother was the local wedding cake maker for the tri-county area. (We're having it today—Mark's sister took over the cake-making when his mom died. It is still delicious.) And I know that even at the time, I thought it wasn't as big of a deal as people were making it.

In terms of academic progress, I was right. But as I watch my niece get ready for college and look at her baby pictures, I get how the transition into adulthood really is in motion. Even as it will take a few years to set in, it's already happening. Amber has 100 rubber ducks wearing graduation hats to fl oat in the pool during the party. I know I didn't have that. Whatever I did have probably involved Dena and our one male friend, Tom, and driving up and down the one-mile main street in my car or Tom's, listening to OMD. I'm sure we didn't think a minute further than the next minute. *Sugar Tax* had just come out. Why would we even need to.

All we knew at eighteen was that freedom was a car and leaving home. We so longed to get away, even as we loved being together, even as we didn't talk about it, even as we lived each day as if we were pirates raiding the day for fun. We felt the energy of OMD without really listening to the lyrics, even as we'd sing them, which is something I hear now from the students that I teach. *We don't listen to our music—we just feel it*. How could we miss the relevance of such lines as these, on the edge of escape from our stifling town:

---

[4] See "I Don't Enjoy the Silence."

119

You say that love will capture me
Not unless you give it free
Sick and tired
don't know why?

Years later, I would read Hanif Abdurraqib's *You Can't Kill Us Until You Kill Us.* In his essay "Under Half-Florescent Lights: The Wonder Years and the Great Suburban Narrative," his narrator bikes through nicer neighborhoods and wonders who lives inside those houses. "I mean," he says, "it creates a longing within the imagination. You long for a place that you know only by its snapshots and not by the lives moving within them. It allowed me to fantasize, imagine a world where everyone was happy and no one ever hurt." Later he says that "[h]ome is where the heart begins, but not where the heart stays."

It's not that we looked enviously towards the future, the college brochures with their pictures of open-mouthed laughs and autumn leaves—we were all too smart and too Gen X to believe in advertised freedom. Instead, I think we knew we had to make the waiting bearable by sailing along on synthesized sound, the synthesizer doing what the verb "synthesize" really means: to bring everything together into sound and sonic texture. Cheerfully, we sang along with OMD: *People try to drag us down / so we learn to swim before we drown.* The bullies, the unkind judgments, the angst and anger that fill the great suburban narrative . . . in a small town, there are no suburbs. The pool is so small, you'd think you couldn't drown, but you could. But you also couldn't swim that far away just yet because you knew exactly who lived in every single house.

That's why you had friends. Friends who loved your music, who felt it, and could make a small trio of friends feel like swimming, small ducks with or without graduation hats.

Later that summer, Tom and I would watch Dena drive off for the last time from my house. "You know it will never be the same," he said. Both he and Dena thought I was the one who would hold on. That hurt me. If anything, I thought I was the one all too aware of the passing of the moment, why I'd turn the music up and sing. Even if I didn't know all the words, I was trying to learn them as we went. *To burn always with this hard, gemlike flame, to maintain this ecstasy, is success in life.*

Maintaining—it doesn't mean "stopping change." It means

"preserving the vitality and presence in the moment."

In twenty years, Dena and Tom and I all lived on the West Coast. We never went to see each other.

If we had, I would like to think we could listen to this music and they wouldn't think I was trying to "recapture" a moment that was gone. Music is, always, both time travel and beyond time itself.

One night, OMD was in town, playing the Showbox, a Seattle music venue so old going there is itself a form of time travel. I bought a last-minute ticket and cried all the way through "Souvenir." Put it on now, and think of three high school friends who helped each other through the time their hearts began:

All I need is
Co-ordination
I can't imagine
My destination
My intention
Ask my opinion
But no excuse
My feelings still remain

Bob Casale, "Bob 2," of Devo died at age 61. I was ten when my sister Amber was sixteen, and, forbidden to enter her bedroom, it was an act of bravery and necessity when I'd sneak into her room to listen to Devo's *This Is Devo* on her record player. What child wouldn't take "time out for fun," be completely entranced by these strange men in their red flowerpot hats? Though I was not in their target audience, I had that most powerful of all forces shaping me: a cool older sister.

But my sister and I define "closeness," as many sisters do, in complicated ways. I could say that we are close in that we share a range of comic facial expressions only we find hilarious. We can guess the joke the other one is heading for at any given moment, when one person's rhythmic tapping on the table is the cue for the other to tap the bass line to "Ooo-de-lah-lee" from the fox *Robin Hood*. Last month, she texted me a list of complaints my mom made during their trip to Kansas City: "I don't like bagels—too doughy," "I don't like English muffins—I shouldn't have ordered them." I punctuated the best ones with a volley of laughing cat face emojis.

I could also say we are not close because of the many ways in which we are different, in all the most stereotypical ways. I left for the city, while she stayed in our hometown in Kansas. She got married and had two children, while I went to graduate school[5]. More painfully, I could say we are not close because my dad pitted us against each other, and putting me down, mocking my "spacy-ness," was one way to win points with him. Once, when visiting me in Seattle, she saw the book *The Girl with the Dragon Tattoo* on a friend's bookshelf. Turning to my friend, Amber asked, casually, "Don't you think that girl is SO much like Bryn?" "She's a . . . sociopath," replied my baffled friend. (I have no tattoos and can do almost nothing with computers, for the record.) One of our greatest bonding experiences was when, drunk on some alcoholic version of a cherry limeade, she confessed to me that at one point, Dad had written both of us, the daughters, out of his will. "I mean, I could understand *you*," she said, swaying forward over the table earnestly, "but *me*?" I agreed solemnly, unsurprised, unhurt. We'd accepted our roles long, long ago. It is the duty of sisters to recognize they aren't our fault.

---

[5] Since the writing of this essay, my sister is now Dr. Amber Miller, finishing her EdD well before I finished this book. That is also a difference between us: she doesn't stop until she's done. I stop for snacks. A lot. Ok, she stops for snacks, too.

Of course, these differences generate conflicts over the years, and I know I am also to blame. Amber would say we are not closer because I am terrible at calling and miss all the important life events of our family since I moved away. I send presents late or not at all. We are distant, in ways both physical and emotional, and because she is five years older, we weren't as intimate as many sisters growing up. The trust just wasn't there. Stay out of my room, she ordered. *Stay away from my heart, I'd think.*

But grow up together we did, and, like catching the flu, influence is often spread by sheer proximity. There was always, always music in our house: we all sang, played piano, played flute. My mom would play Berlioz's "Dream of a Witches' Sabbath" and I would hide in terror when I was four; later, as a teenager, I would listen to the *Out of Africa* soundtrack with her and know my mother was lonely. My dad sang, too, but silly songs, songs I thought, for years, he had made up: Gene Autry's "Here Comes Peter Cottontail," Fess Parker's "Wringle Wran-gle," which I realize now would foretell our own angry conflicts after my parents' divorce, when I was expected, at sixteen, to take over as house-keeper and cook: *Wringle wrangle / jingy jong jangle / I've got me a purdy woman's love / got a dollar's worth of beans / and a new pair of jeans / got a woman to cook / and wash and things.* Amber's musical influence had less to do with emotional connection than with thin walls and access to her record player. She would dress like Jennifer Beals in Flash Dance and go to pompon practice. I'd sneak in, wearing glasses and my dorky sweater vests, and listen to Asia, to Foreigner, to Taste of Honey's cover of "Sukiyaki." But most of all, I listened to Devo. At age ten, in Kansas, what could be stranger, sillier, more fun to dance to, more intriguing? Who were these men? What were men? Were they Devo? If so, and my sister liked them, did she understand them—Devo, men? If she liked them and I liked them, did that mean that somehow, on some level, she understood me?

I speak of my sister's musical influence as one always speaks of influence: in the past tense. Now, she thinks my music is boring; I think hers sucks. As with fashion, Amber likes whatever is new; I search through thrift stores for whatever seems connected to the past or inter-esting for the future. We have a new car game where she'll play a song I've never heard, and I guess "It's Pink" every time. (I'm usually right.) I've come to terms with the non-stop Mariah Carey Christmas album every Christmas, which is the only time I'm home now. I favor walls of guitar or atmospheric dream pop, which, even my young niece, my sister's child, informs me, doesn't have enough "beat." Though we are both strong singers, when I am at home, she always beats me at Guitar Hero or Glee karaoke because I simply do not know any of those songs in the fashion required. You have to sing "Don't Stop Believing" exactly as some character sings it, and they just don't have an "indie" version of those games yet.

But this is why I love my sister, and why I know we still count for each other: she loves music. Really, really loves it. My big sister taught elementary school music for years, and her Christmas programs were creative, engaging. Once, she put on a Christmas musical called *Elfis*, complete with an Elvis-impersonator elf and hula-dancing reindeer. I laughed so hard and so long that my brother-in-law nudged me to knock it off. Children would follow Amber around town, as if she were a more benevolent Pied Piper, waving excitedly at her in the grocery store. "Hi, Mrs. Miller!" they'd squeak. When she quit for upper administration, she bemoaned the decision over the phone to me. "But this new job could be a great opportunity for you," I said. "Nooooooooo!" she wailed. "I want to sing and dance and roll on the ground, like I did in my old job!"

She loves music. And even if it means a very Celine Dion Christmas, I can appreciate her need for 24-hour sound, the way, sometimes, music replaces intimacy and gives voice to the things sisters cannot say to one another, a lyrical punchline to a musical joke.

And once, there was music we shared. My first taste of "cool" came from listening to her Devo records, and Devo still captures best why I insist we will always be, sometimes, close: like us, they were funny, they were fun, and they were weird.

We are Devo.

The Undertaker's Son was my first real boyfriend, and he was a wonderful first real boyfriend, although, like my sister now, his taste in music was sometimes questionable. He favored bands like Color Me Badd and, on his first mixed tape for me, there were several songs by The Party—the Mickey Mouse Club Band of the time. He was a Pisces, so, in many ways, this mawkish sentimentality made sense: all of my Piscean friends can cry on a dime. Though it came out at least 15 years after we dated, I would not hesitate to bet good money that he loved *The Notebook*. But it totally worked out for me—at seventeen, we were of that glorious age when finally, one can do for a sweetheart all the most romantic things one's seen in movies. The Undertaker's Son was the kind of boyfriend who bought you a dozen roses "just because." I can only imagine the number of hours he'd had to work washing cars at the local dealership to make the money.

He dressed up in a town where men only noticed which state university was on their sweatshirt. He liked his mom. He had female friends who were just friends. He had some sense of manners, didn't chew tobacco, and didn't plan on staying in our town or joining the family mortuary business. Yet, though our entire high school had only 120 students, I'd never really noticed him before somehow. But when we fell in love, it made sense: I wore heels for no reason, abhorred toxic masculinity before it was a term, and I also didn't want this town.

Moreover, The Undertaker's Son didn't fear my difference. This sounds like a cliché, but it's one that can never be meaningless if you were a young girl, mocked and antagonized by the opposite sex in your teen years. When friends who grew up in cities try to understand my rural high school experiences, they can't: they had drama class, dance studios, other friends who wore black. The best they can do is to over-simplify—they assume I hated every moment. But I was a cheerleader, the lead in the musical each year. (Our school only did one a year—that was the drama department.) I had close friends and laughed. I wasn't not liked. But I was smart, and I was not amused by the low-ball humor, the disdain for education, for school, the anti-feminist attitude of most boys I encountered. The most common exchange between me and a boy was a taunting comment from him, followed by a haughty silence or a cutting retort from me. "What's wrong with your friend?" a boy once asked my friend, as we cruised Main Street in his car. (I'd been silent for several minutes as the girls laughed at the boys' sexist jokes.) "Nothing's wrong with me," I said. "I just don't think you're funny."

So when this kind, funny, blonde boy, some kind of Duckie from *Pretty in Pink*, with his mouse-like face and a confidence I'd never noticed, pursued me one night at the musical cast party (it was an overnight lock-in—it's like they wanted us to hook up), it wasn't just a flirtation for me. I had the rare sense of being recognized and, moreover, appreciated. Desired. Seen. The Undertaker's Son later told me he'd told his mom he was going to ask me out, and she was delighted. "Oh, I've always thought she seemed neat!" she said. I was used to that from moms—but not from their sons.

He was, however, like all Pisceans, two fish swimming in opposite directions: different but conventional, open but full of secrets, committed but prone to wandering. Years later, when he *did* end up becoming a mortician, I wasn't fully surprised: resolve and willfulness aren't particularly Piscean traits, and tendencies towards uncertainty and accommodation are. I think now of my favorite Beatle, George Harrison, another Pisces, the spiritual one, the one most committed to meditation, the man who wrote "Something," the song Frank Sinatra called the "most romantic song in English." In the bridge, Harrison sings, with a conviction that belies the lyrics' ambivalence: *You're asking me will our love grow / I don't know / I don't know.* I've come to wonder in later years, how romantic that really is: yet another woman trying to get her man to open up, commit, communicate, getting only a vague response, however sincere. "Something" was written for Patti Boyd, Harrison's first wife, with whom he fell in love on the set of *A Hard Day's Night*. She is one of the schoolgirls on the train in the first scene, another girl surprised by the boy overshadowed by the more ego-driven John and the sweet-faced Paul. Patti will later leave George for Eric Clapton, but before she does, Clapton will write "Layla" for her: "Layla"—the passionate antidote to the reflective, if poetic uncertainty of "Something."

In my young romance, the Piscean ambivalence manifested painfully. The Undertaker's Son eventually cheated on me with a girl from Methodist Leadership Camp, and I would struggle for years to learn the great lesson of my love life: to choose the man who tells me *you've got me on my knees / I'm begging, darling, please,* instead of wistfully waiting for the boy who tells me *there's something in the way [I] move.* To know that choices, not words, are the proof of love.

But before I learned that, I loved the romantic words, words, words. Patti also inspires "Wonderful Tonight," which appears on that same first mixed tape with Color Me Badd and The Party. I played the tape on repeat all for weeks. And you'd think, loving George Harrison as I do, that because "Clapton" brings up "cheating," the song would have been ruined for me. Instead, it reminds me of that George-like, Piscean gentleness, of that first sense of romantic approval, that sense of being a woman who, like Patti, inspired both tenderness and searing passion. George Harrison forgave Eric Clapton for the sake of greater music, and when Harrison died, Clapton honored that forgiveness, directing and performing in the Concert for George. A good song is a good song, and any love beautifully expressed can never have been wholly empty.

The Undertaker's Son and I broke up and never did anything together again, ever. From that point on, until the end of my twenties, I would cheat on nearly every boyfriend to come, a pre-emptive strike to protect myself from that early breach of trust. But once, when I was home visiting from college, I attended a high school event in which he had convinced three other boys to dress in drag and lip sync En Vogue's "Giving Him Something He Can Feel." He was the lead singer and wore a slinky red dress, his performance silly and perfect, all at the same time. It was really Something. It was exactly the kind of thing I had liked about him, a way of being different and honoring difference that eventually settled into something wonderful—tonight and in all the other nights I think of love shared and lost. It felt something like forgiveness.

Here's a poem for Patti.

Patti of the World's Two Greatest Love Songs

In the movie where you'll meet him,
you are a silent, doll-eyed nobody,
smiling sweetly in the dining car,
the only jumpered schoolgirl to make it past
the fencing
to the Beatles and the baggage.
He just smiles at you once.

I watch this part again and over,
looking for the something
in the way you move,
how you would ease a worried mind.

Each time, I only see your eyes,
the lashes that were surely fake,
stuck on at a time when Twiggy was queen
and you were on her runway;
silence moving next to stars, you were
a comet's path or an asteroid.

Is it your own destruction
or the way that you destroy?
The one, my idol, never one for begging,
just asked you to stay, his only human mystery
amid concerts and sitars, groggy fame, detachment,
the song Sinatra called the most romantic song in English—not enough
to keep you there, the Something
only powerful to those who didn't know you.

Maybe you wanted more —the quiet one
Mumbling his mantras—soulful, yes, but
inarticulate and mute about
what it was you were to him,
other than merely Something.

Maybe
the sight of someone begging
on their knees,
no pride, ethics crumbling like
sugar paste
beneath your tangled lashes,
or whatever else it is that
I can't see in the dining car,
is the better measure of love,

the love that lets you know
it's You he wants—even if he calls you Layla—
that he will not be at peace if he cannot have you,
that you are not like all things, which must pass,
that you he will struggle for,
that desire is not to be denied,
that sometimes, Something
isn't better than nothing.

128

These Arms Were Mine: First Love is a Slow Dance that Goes on Forever, or, An Attempt to Forgive a History of Us in Debt

There are stories one needs to tell again and again, turning them over and through, like cloth in a river, rubbing and rub-bing until it comes clean. Let me tell this again and take out the shame and the grief, the stain of the anger—not because they are not there but because they are only a part of the fabric. Let me tell this story again, to myself and to you, to find mercy for us both.

First Love looks like so many things. For my niece, right now, it looks like a tall, silent guy being forced to make Smores and endure her mother's and aunt's incessant, quick-paced, ludicrous banter and badgering. For my sister, it looked like a 19-year-old girl driving across the state of Kansas every weekend to see the guy she started dating the summer before her first year of college, the guy to whom she would become engaged at the end of that year. I don't know if I really saw my first love as my First Love, until years passed[6] and I realized he was still the one I thought of, when I think of young love.

For one thing, he was too young for me. At an age when half a year develops the brain substantially, he was four years younger, though I wouldn't know that at first. We met at musical theatre camp (*I know*), and he followed me around a lot. New to kissing, I was not averse to doing more of it, even if I wasn't sure about this kid who liked to talk about horror movies and was definitely in charge of finding out how to get marijuana from the college-age stagehands.

After that first week of making out behind the sets, he only called me once, and that pattern continued: once a year. Because, like some fabled creature reborn under magical conditions, or a plant that blooms only when two blue moons follow each other, this attraction renewed itself every year.

For 6 years.

We made out behind sets, found unused rooms with broken pianos in the fine arts center, until I graduated from high school—and then I was a counselor, attending the college where the camp was held, which meant I knew more unused rooms, more places dark and intimate. At

[6] See also "A History of Us in Debt."

the camp dance, when Otis Redding's "These Arms of Mine" came on, he walked across the room, and we danced like we were dissolving into each other, to the confusion and discomfort of the whole camp, I'm sure—or at least those who didn't know this happened every year. His eyes shone with the focused heat of anyone forbidden anything, but especially passion. Old enough to question everything, I somehow accepted, without question, that while everything else was up for intellectual grabs, this was fate. Even if he never wrote me, never called me, I was going to suffer and wait it out.

Until he was . . . what? Old enough? Old enough for what?

Real relationships in college came and went.

Its highest point was followed, quickly, by its lowest point[7] when he sat me down and tried to get me to see there was no future for this strange, passionate thing that seemed like fate, or maybe love. "We're worse than opposites, Bryn," he said, pulling his hands apart and bringing them close together but not touching. "We're like . . . this." His hands hovered apart, like a game of cat's cradle without any string. And he was right—age isn't everything, but it can be like string.

So, I set myself to the task of undoing my naive beliefs about love and fate and, for more than a few months, the meaning of life. It took a few years. I stopped reading Jung.

We finally did reconnect, after 11 years, and while we weren't actively close, I found his presence in my life added a depth and richness akin to that of a childhood friend, a cherished family member who lives far away. He still never made me a CD or tape, never wrote me a letter, and the only picture I have of him is the double of one another counselor gave me of him with another girl.

That is why this song, "These Arms of Mine," is a slow dance I can still feel 22 years later. It holds a weight in my heart so heavy that if my heart was an ocean, which I sometimes believe it is, this love would be anchored to its very floor. It's the only thing I feel like I really have from him. He even goes by a different name these days, but once he texted me this, before he lost me to his drinking forever: "I'm in a bar, and 'These Arms of Mine' just came on, and I'm 16 years old." It felt good to know then that he too could feel lost in that moment with me, once again that boy I know now I really loved.

---

[7] That is, the lowest point until at age 40, I saw him as an adult—again, see "A History of Us in Debt."

(Hidden Track)
The Summer We Knew We Were Young

As each summer draws nigh, and my students make their summer living situations with each other, I miss so deeply the house in which I lived the summer between my junior and senior years of college. For reasons I asked to know, it was called the Baumgartner House, a pink Craftsman Bungalow with a big front porch, built-in bookshelves, and an electrical system so dangerously old that when you ground coffee, the light would flicker. I lived in it with Lost Lila Moore[8] and my friend Liz, who would fall in love with her future husband all of that summer, leaving me the ten-window bedroom all to myself. Our friends the DJ Muppet[9], his best friend Stephan, and a loaner-cat named Honey lived in the basement.

We all played guitar.

We all had jobs we liked but didn't really care about: I was re-painting the college a shade called "Industrial Almond," Liz did something relatively meaningful, though I can't remember what, and Lila was the cool Godfather's Delivery Girl Who Drove a Red Convertible. She came home from work one day and told us, with tears of laughter, of the six- year-old's birthday party to which she'd delivered that day. When they saw her car, the birthday girl had exclaimed, "When I grow up, I'm gonna have a car like that. And when I grow up, I wanna be the Pizza Girl!"

Everyone came over to that house that summer. Since my job started early, I'd come home at 3:00 to find half our friend group already on the porch, playing Uno and drinking beer. We spent Lila's tip money on bags of cherries and would eat them all, driving around in her convertible, belting "American Girl." I kissed The German Mennonite for what I thought was the last time outside of that house. One night, both floors of the house stayed up and watched somewhere between four to eight hours of Sting / the Police videos. Sting was a still a minor religious icon in the mid-90s, even though he was walking in fields of gold instead of having tea in the Sahara, and we loved how he'd say "Hurt me, baby" after the bridge of "Every Step You Take." When I got the letter from The German Mennonite[10] announcing he was going

---

8 See "Searching for Lila Moore."

9 See "The Muppet and the Dreamer"

10 See "Message in a Bottle."

to date that other Mennonite girl, I went out into the living room where everyone was gathered, cried, and told them, then said "I'm hot—hand me the scissors." I sat in front of the mirror and cut off my waist-long hair to my chin, while they cheered. I sent him a piece of it. They cheered again.

Every day was tomato and mustard sandwiches, wearing each other's dresses, spontaneously driving to Oklahoma City. Every night was the pleasure of fresh bread, the solace of friends when a lover was lost, the coming in covered with mosquito bites from making out in the warm Kansas eve. Everyone could sing every song on Nanci Griffith's *Other Voices, Other Rooms*, and even as we'd brush our teeth, we could hear all the other voices sing in all the other rooms.

Moving out was chaotic, as any disruption of paradise should be. Honey the Cat had a terrible case of fleas, with which we'd coped temporarily by wearing thick woolen socks when we went down to get the laundry. On moving day, though, we had to pull mattresses out, flea-bomb the whole place, swearing at the friend who'd foisted Honey off on us for the summer, and hating the poisons tainting the end of this glorious tenure.

We all moved back into the modular apartments on campus, probably 500 yards away. The family from whom we'd sublet the house moved back in, and summer was gone.

I knew while I was there that I would never have another summer so golden in my life—that it had been the most perfect expression of being young and hopeful and free. Every day, that knowledge both saddened me and made me that much more committed to being as intimate with the moments of that house as I possibly could. I would later find a term for this: "anticipatory nostalgia." I miss things even before they are gone.

If you find that tragic, you are wrong. That awareness, that imminent sadness, etched that summer into me like light fixes the image on a photographic plate, so deeply that I can call up my twenty-year-old self, as I near my 50th birthday, as easily as clear water from a stream.

Easier—and with more pleasure. And with so much more inside of it than words.

We listened to Kate Wolf a lot, and "Cornflower Blue" was our house song. It's the kind of music to which I no longer listen much, the music of that young woman I was just becoming, in that time of infinite ease and gladness. I wonder about this a lot—why I can't give myself to folk music like I used to. Sometimes I blame Seattle: so non-sentimental, so "cool," so quick to mislabel kindness as naivete. And it's true that, for folk music, you need your community to share it with you, or its aching sincerity will crush you as you note the gap between its world and your own, so snide, so cool, so unkind. Folk music is meant to be sung together, from room to room, with other voices. Still, knowing I can hear my own young voice so clearly among those sometimes helps me know I come from that source of love and hope, that, like the song, what we come from and feed ourselves with gives us a way of seeing and feeling that never really goes away: *Cornflower blue / bloomin' in the mornin' sun / Tiny flowers that grew / from when our love had just begun.*

Kate Wolf died at 44 from leukemia, four years younger than me now. Even at 21, we knew that was too young. It seems fitting that the only videos I find of the song on YouTube are merely still-life pictures of cornflowers or of her album cover. Even though the music video took off in 1981 with "Video Killed the Radio Star," folk music videos were, as they are still, disinterested in keeping up with the times, content to be on the radio, maybe not even showing the star. Those vid-eos are so terribly pure, so incredibly innocent in their low-production value, they could not more perfectly represent the summer I knew I was young. But they are high quality enough for me to replay in my mind, whenever I need.

If love came in colors, then I'd choose this one for you.

Everybody Got Their Something, or Pray Someone Steals Your
College Music Soon

I know. I know at first, you'll walk into your bedroom and your face will fall: the empty CD racks. I know you'll feel upset when nothing in the rest of the house was taken, not even all the laptops our roommate Dan works on in the living room, the ones that you and I keep telling him to keep in his own space. I know you know we feel it too, as we gather around you in that room—no one wants to lose their past to a stranger searching a house for something to quickly sell. No one wants to know your old heart can't be traced just because it has no serial num-ber.

I know you will be glad I chased the robber down the hall into the yard but also glad I didn't catch him—what would I have done? I know we'll all think it is funny the thief also stole Dan's backpack and dumped its contents on your bed, especially when you hold up the purple underwear and say, "Whose are THESE?" I know it is still funny when Dan sheepishly says, "They're mine." I know we'll all rejoice when you remember you're the only one with renter's insurance. I know I didn't even know that such a thing existed, since I barely make a living. I know I'll think right then that you're a woman of great resourcefulness.

I know we'll look at the check insurance sends you in awe: $1000, and I will love you all the more when you say you're going to use it all on rebuilding your music collection. I know that every time we go to Sonic Boom, Cellophane Square, or Orpheum, you will cock your ear and ask the record clerk "What's that?" I know we'll look at each other and buy bands we've never heard of: Mint Royale, ICU, Propellerheads, Thom Yorke.

I know we'll both get tired of Dan and all the laptops and the fact I couldn't tell, at first, if we were being robbed or if there was just another scraggly guy crashing at our house, without us being told. I know that we become best friends during this time and that the house we move into together, just the two of us, is really our first home. I know we'll dance to the Propellerheads' song "Velvet Pants" and go in search of some ourselves. I know the salesgirl will misunderstand us and think that we say "final pants," and I know that after we leave that store, we'll plan "The Final Pants" party and go buy music just for it. I know your favorite purchase will be Nikka Costa's "Everybody Got Their Something."

I know we'll spill a million drinks on the tile floor of the orange kitchen and make pie while singing Tom Petty, and you'll do your funny dance that looks like playing maracas. I know I'll listen to you make up songs about banana slugs for the nature day camp at which you work, even though you don't sing well. "It's to the tune of 'La Bamba!'" you'll say, and I'll pretend to hear that.

And later I know you will move to Austin, and we'll go to SXSW each year in search of other drinks to spill and other bands to love. I know we'll make bigger mistakes and hurt ourselves and CDs will disappear, and I'll date an alcoholic and have tumors in my head, and you will stop eating, and I'll have to tell you to stop stopping. I know your boyfriend will not get us, think we both just need to talk all the time without ever really listening, and I know that I will hate him for that.

But I also know you'll buy me a tiny speaker on which to stream music, make me a mix for my radiation treatments, break up with the boyfriend. I know I will call you every week, make you funny tee shirts with the names of favorite snacks on them, tell our friends here that everybody's got their something, even if it's suffering, and that you and I are going to be ok. I know some things are difficult, that taking a friendship across a lifetime means we drop things along the way but that we carry other things together.

I know it isn't fun to lose so much sometimes. I know that. And I know we know how to rebuild, to shift the weight, and how to keep on listening.

Use Your Illusion: Import B-Sides

Ain't That Enough
   Teenage Fanclub, *"Ain't That Enough"*

The DJ Muppet: My Brother, My Sister
   Eric Johnson, *"Forty Mile Town"* and Juliana Hatfield, *"Spin the Bottle"*

No Deal With God

   Kate Bush, *"Running Up that Hill"*

Performance Art's A Kind of Love
   Animal Collective, *"Did You See the Words"*

Ain't That Enough

There's a lot of music I owe to the Record Store Guy because the Record Store Guy was THAT GUY. I worked in the used bookstore; he worked in the used record store across the street. We'd wave at each other through our windows. Back then, I was still listening primarily to folk music; he listened to everything.

Well, almost everything. Our first fight was when I looked through his 300+ CD collection and found one—ONE—CD by a female musician, not counting female back-up singers or bass players in mostly all-male bands. I was finishing my master's program in cultural studies and women's studies, and I accused him of the worst kind of misogyny: the unconscious kind. (To be fair, the one female CD was one by Tori Amos, who kind of counts as 57 women.

For all of that, the Record Store Guy and I had SO MUCH FUN. He made me laugh harder than anyone else, he moved to Seattle with me, and we pulled over on the sides of any road that looked interesting on the way. In the end, we were perhaps too similar and not similar enough: too reactive, too temperamental, a little bit selfish . . . a little bit . . . young. He went on to use his insatiable love of data well: he's a professor, teaching creative non-fiction. He writes about monuments— the whole world is a history of objects for him, which accounts, really, for the justifiable pride he took in his music collection. Before I broke up with him, I would sit down in front of our stacks of CDs and write down every album I would need to repurchase: Stereolab, every Elliot Smith album, an obscure Scottish musician Momus, who had been the first show we went to when we arrived in Seattle. When we were still in love with the possibility of music, love, and ourselves.

We moved our young, selfish, hilarious selves across the country to fight over why he got to use his money for CDs and I got to use mine on dish soap for the house. But on our way, we stopped at his parents' house in Boulder, where his father told us that he thought of us every time he heard that song "The Way" by Fastball: *They made up their minds / and they started packing*. He probably wasn't sure we were doing the right thing, I'll bet, though it seemed he also hoped the best for us. What parent wouldn't worry and what parent wouldn't hope his fresh-faced child has met another fresh-faced child in love and that they are off on adventure, even however brief?

"Ain't That Enough," by Teenage Fanclub, is one of the millions of bands to which the Record Store Guy introduced me, so long ago I forget I didn't know them before I met him. I remember this band years later when I see the movie Young Adult. The narcissistic, disconnected Charlize Theron finds out her high school boyfriend and his wife have had a baby, digs out that boyfriend's mixed tape for her and puts it on "repeat one," driving like a maniac to Teenage Fan Club's "The Concept," hoping to get him back. But the song already holds a warning for her, as it holds for any teenaged fan in love: *I didn't want to hurt you / oooooooh yeaaahhh.*

It didn't make me want to get him back. I hadn't even bothered to repurchase half of what I'd put on that list; sometimes, you just need to take the notes of what you had with you. But that movie brought me back to "Ain't That Enough," and, as the song says, the days that found you. At that time, in our early twenties, the good days just flooded in, one after another, like sparkling ripples of heat or ocean water. Love waved a friendly hand and reached out, an 82-degree day in February, a perfect British pop song dressed in nerdy-adorable thrift store jumpers, and you dropped what you were doing and ran outside to be with it.

I watched the video of the song for the first time recently, and I can see so easily why we never see our own looming problems in our early love relationships—the guitars jangle, the bandmates are beaming; they look out on the ocean, and the sun shines on them so brightly there will never, ever be clouds. How startling to see how much the twenty-some year-old Record Store Guy looked like most of the band. Throughout the video, shots of them by the ocean alternate with images of a swimming pool, "no diving" prominently visible. Signs must have been a focus in the video, since there are so many, many signs, but "no diving" and "one way" are potent in that they are the only ones expressing limits. Despite them, you also see a woman swimming strongly. Then children jumping gleefully on a trampoline, hurling their bodies towards the event of moving up. This is the power and beauty of youth. No Diving means Jump. *Time can only make demands / Fill it up with grains of sand / Bring your loving over.* Near the end, a band member stands behind the "one way" sign and dances, so he looks like a bobble-headed stick figure of joy and headlong focus on the future. Many of us can only notice the signs right in front of our faces, but maybe that's ok. It keeps us in the present.

"Ain't that Enough" is a monument to a drive across the country to a new, bright, young, urban life—full of promise, sure to be unfulfilled by each other, posing like young rock stars when the show's only begun, leaving the show clutching the set lists of all those days and nights.

140

The DJ Muppet: My Brother, My Sister

Today, I woke up with Eric Johnson's "Forty Mile Town" in my head. It is a song, I might add, to which I have not listened since college. I won't insist you listen to it, as I would, say, Kate Bush's "Running Up that Hill" or the Arcade Fire's "Neighborhood #3." Twenty-three years later, it seems schmaltzier, less beautiful . . . and this is coming from someone who loves, LOVES, the Christopher Cross song "Sailing." But when you're thinking about people to whom you were once much closer, it seems, for me, that brings up two categories of people, mostly: college friends and former lovers.

The DJ Muppet was kind of both. "Quick," I texted my friend J. E. once, as adults, "why is ___ a Muppet?" The text shot back: "Big feathery poof of hair. Giant arm movements as if there were rods attached to his hands. So Loud." DJ Muppet was hilarious, I am hilarious, so we briefly dated and were terrible, terrible, horrible together: crabby and cranky and unpredictable. So, we stopped and happily spent the rest of our college years together in plays, musicals, choir concerts, radio shows, classes, and, for one summer, as housemates[11]. When I was in a David Mamet play and had to play a chain smoker; the DJ Muppet took me out back of the fine arts center and taught me how to smoke. He took great pleasure in it—particularly because I didn't. "Oh my GOD, Brynny!! You are the worst smoker!!!" he'd scream.

The DJ Muppet loved screaming. The DJ Muppet had an Irish fisherman's sweater about which my mom still speaks fondly. The DJ Muppet was the leader of a pack of wild Lost Boys and was responsible for some of the more ridiculous pranks on campus, always involving large phallic structures. Other times, he'd sulk and grumble, less playful Muppet and more like Sweetums, the sensitive monster. "He's in a mood," we'd whisper. And then he'd bring you the Enya Christmas EP he stole from the radio station.

We were both DJs at that college radio station and spent many silly hours in the booth together singing very, very loudly and intentionally not that well. Our favorite was Juliana Hatfield's "Spin the Bottle." We nearly broke equipment bouncing around the booth. How 90s is that?

In reality, the DJ Muppet had a beautiful singing voice, and he married another dear friend, also with a beautiful singing voice. They

---

[11] See "The Summer We Knew We Were Young."

have a million long-limbed boy children now, a new pack of Lost Boys to lead.

The last time I saw the DJ Muppet, it had been years, and I was visiting with his wife in their house swhen he came home for dinner. "HI!" I bounded towards him. "Oh, hi, Brynny," he said, hanging up his coat and walking into the next room, away from me. For some people, you're always the irritating little sister, sometimes enlisted in the hijinks, sometimes merely tolerated. Juliana Hatfield sings, in another song of hers, about sisters with a similar dynamic:

> *She's got a wall around her nobody can climb.*
> *She lets her ladder down for those who really shine. I tried to*
> *scale it, but to me she's blind.*

But the DJ Muppet, like so many men I was privileged to befriend in college, was the kind of brother I needed: the kind who didn't need anything from you but your silliest company, who gave you all the space you needed while still giving a damn, the kind whose sensitivity sometimes helped them see your own, the sweetest voice with the smoker's edge.

I had a popcorn cake for, I think, my seventh birthday. Or ninth. It was good—think "Bundt cake-shaped popcorn ball, with M and M's." Popcorn cake is in that category of Midwestern "delights" you try to make for a coastal potluck, years later, and can't believe you ever ate multiple pieces of something that sweet.

The lesson: One big hit does not equal a lifetime of love.

Jerry Seinfeld puts it another way:

> *Of course, when you're a kid, you can be friends with anybody. Re-member when you were a little kid—what were the qualifications? If someone's in front of my house NOW, That's my friend, they're my friend. That's it. Are you a grown-up? No. Great! Come on in. Jump up and down on my bed. And if you have anything in common at all . . . You like Cherry Soda? I like Cherry Soda! We'll be best friends!*

I still do that. I offer my love for a song, literally, pretty often.

Once, when I was at Kansas State, getting my master's degree, a guy drove me out into the country and played me Kate Bush's "Running Up that Hill," while we lay on the warm car hood under stars, while a cool summer breeze blew over us. Feel that for a moment. It was the first time I'd heard the song. He reached out for my hand.

If you didn't fall in love, then, too, you are made of stone.

Other times, I lose my heart to a sentence a student writes, showing they are moved and changed by something beautiful in the world, or to a sympathetic look someone gives you at a party; you think, "They don't know me at all, but they get me," and trust in the world expands like the shades of sunrise stretching up and out across the sky. One of my all-time favorite students, the preternaturally wise Nicolene, told me she once deeply bonded with a boy over a misread line in The Catcher in the Rye. My own best friend from high school Dena and I often ended conversations about the universe like this:

"You know?"

"Yeah, I know."

As if tacit understanding was all you needed.

But sometimes, it is. When we tell these stories where our hearts fling themselves outwards like unattended children, why is the implicit moral "so then, don't do that again"? Don't mistake music for intimacy. Don't attach too much to intuitive responses. Don't think someone can understand you just because they share your love of truth and beauty, vastness and the stars.

It's true the "Running Up that Hill" Guy wasn't as spiritual as I'd assumed he was. He just turned out to be a conflicted Christian. And it's also true that the student's beautiful sentence doesn't always bespeak a complex intellect and struggling soul. Sometimes it just means they can't spell, as when a student described an architect as "the soul design-er." And sometimes, maybe someone isn't a very good reader, needing guidance so badly they will it up from the page, rearranging letters and altering syntax until a mistake looks like a miracle[12].

But I don't care. I think I can count on one hand—maybe even one finger—the times those connections really weren't worth it. Is it really wisdom to start mistrusting the deeply felt experience, those small and precious offerings, the tiny gestures that reach you, even if that person wasn't reaching out? Are you shallow if you respond equally to a shared secret and popcorn cake?

I once told a British literature class that I had started watching *Game of Thrones*. Later that week, one of them was talking about Heathcliff or Hareton and how he was both part of the family, yet not part of the family, and I said, "So, he's a Greyjoy?" They erupted in laughter. I swear to God (on all the gods that be, running up and down their hills) class became even better, even livelier because of that one moment. It led ultimately to me showing them the video of Kate Bush singing "Wuthering Heights." The responses were mixed. "So, like, this was a big hit, huh? Like, people were jamming out to this on boom-boxes?" asked David, bemused. "That is the whole gypsy chic look I am GOING FOR," Theresa murmured darkly, in love with this strange and beautiful creature, bending over backwards in unironic interpretive dance, beckoning through her ghost spirit to your willing, waiting heart.

When *Hounds of Love* came out in 1985, Kate Bush wanted to call "Running Up That Hill" something else. She wanted to call it "Deal with God," but her producers worried others would misinterpret the

---

[12] See "Message in a Bottle."

song and block it. In an 1992 interview with Radio 1, Bush says what she wanted was

> *to say that, really, a man and a woman can't understand each other because we are a man and a woman. And if we could actually swap each other's roles, if we could actually be in each other's place for a while, I think we'd both be very surprised! [. . . .] And I think it would lead to a greater understanding. And really the only way I could think it could be done was either . . . you know, I thought a deal with the devil, you know. And I thought, 'Well, no, why not a deal with God!' You know, because in a way it's so much more powerful the whole idea of asking God to make a deal with you. You see, for me it is still called 'Deal with God'; that was its title. But we were told that if we kept this title that it would not be played in any of the religious countries, Italy wouldn't play it, France wouldn't play it, and Australia wouldn't play it! Ireland wouldn't play it, and that generally we might get it blacked purely because it had God in the title.*

So, God stayed in the title as a parenthetical, but for some of us, Kate Bush included, "Deal with God" is the real focus. Not the action of running itself when everything is understood, but the gesture that invites in mystery.

Even as an atheist, I want this: to embrace misunderstandings that draw us towards each other, the imperfect understandings that keep us vulnerable and ready to connect. This is why I was never punk rock—I could never possess its aggressive certainty, feel its anger as liberation, would rather be reeled into wonder than rebel. But that doesn't mean I'm sleeping, unaware. I love the Ramones song, and I don't wanna be sedated, not now or ever. I want to be ignited—even by the tiniest of matches, even if, like Hans Christen Anderson's "The Little Match Girl," the flame burns out quickly. She is left colder than before and dies when her matches run out, but she saw something that looked like love before she did.

I will never run out of matches. I will run up that hill forever, ready to make a deal.

Performance Art's a Kind of Love

The Performance Artist was a man of many . . . men. The child of immigrants, he'd grown up in the land of Kurt Cobain but listened to Steven Sondheim. He went to West Point, worked as an engineer, and then got an MBA, but he also recorded albums of sweet and weird love songs with haunting lines like *I wish I could contain small things / like oceans / or my heart*. He hosted a wildly popular recurring spectacle of an event in which he and his motley crew would choose two local rock stars, interview a random audience crowd member, and then challenge the rock stars to write a song about that interview, all while simultane-ously getting wasted and fending off random and spontaneous audience challenges. My favorite was when they quickly passed out plastic cocktail swords, shouted "Capulet versus Montague!" and audience members commenced with tiny sword fights. At another show, swept up in the crowd's hysteria, I took my top off. (I did that one other time in public, but it was because I was hot from dancing. This time was fueled by pure crowd participation mania.) That show was a supreme mixture of high-brow / low-brow culture: Yoko Ono meets Red Robin.

The Performance Artist loved Yoko Ono. He was, I think, the only boyfriend I ever had who was not in love me. Even now, I wonder, "Was he really ever mine?"

I mean, sure, he once proposed to me over dinner. We'd been speaking of another friend's impending marriage, and the Performance Artist threw down his fork like a gauntlet.

"You wanna get married? Let's get married. Why not? I mean, I love you, and you're pretty and smart, and . . .."

"But you're not in love with me."

"But I love you. We'd be ok. Name the date. Pull the trigger."

"Dude, not only did you just say 'pull the trigger,' as if marrying me would be the end of your natural life, but do you realize that if I changed my name, which I wouldn't, I would be 'Bryn Yin'?"

He'd never thought of that.

But still, the Performance Artist came over immediately when my dad died, and once he blew off a rehearsal to order in sushi with me when I was crying because I found out the Quiet One[13] got married, and, true, he did drive three days with me from Seattle, Washington, to

---

[13] See "A Song with No Words for a Love that Could Not Speak Its Name."

Maryville, Missouri, moving me there to be a professor, trying to keep my spirits up as I left everything I'd loved for years, including him, probably for good. We drove and drove and had an hour-long conversation about how masterfully the Beatles layered vocal tracks on "Because" and how equally masterful it was that Modest Mouse's layers were always slightly uneven. Looking through the CDs he'd brought, as we left Missoula, Montana, I pulled out one with drawings of children and chicken-scratchy penned writing on the front, Animal Collective's Feels.

"How's this one?"

"Bryn, I don't LISTEN to music—I STUDY it. Put it on."

Layers, in geology, mean that one time is the foundation of another. One epoch's detritus mixes with its treasures, pressed into clay or resin or against wet limestone, and something hardens, petrifies, fossilizes. And relationships can be like that: making their marks on us in indelible, permanent ways. But some people, like some moments, aren't meant for keeping or marking. They press against our hearts without invading them or hurting them, or they glitter before us like spectacles of majesty—the light over the Grand Canyon at dusk, not its stony depths.

So let me tell you, there is NO better listening landscape for Animal Collective's Feels than the broad, broad, vast, expansive, open skies of Montana, where the horizon recedes infinitely, and you start to feel like you have nowhere to get to, nowhere to go, nothing but the beauty of that moment filling and filling you like an infinite cup of gladness. The first song, "Did You See the Words Today," opens with piano tinkling like glass, but soon there is a rumbling, as when distant thunder and a rising wind ripple tall grasses, sending waves of electricity skittering, drops of water on a skillet. The thrumming builds, and Avey Tare's voice introduces possibility, an idea to consider: that X next to Y equals a sonic landslide of love as a child on a rollercoaster, screaming. Then the release comes, and that idea is no longer possibility but fact for the moment. All things rise and then converge, and the song rises and descends like a rollercoaster; even the singers' voices mimic the wildness of that ride, with yelps of exultation and long sighs of release. We listened to the whole album in a similar state, only breaking silence occasionally to say "Oh, THAT'S interesting," or "Oooo! That's good!" "Geologist" is even the DJ name of one of the members of the band.

The Performance Artist and I were never in love, but we were near it, which has its own benefits. There's a kind of heightened attention, a state of presence with the other both immersive and critically distant. This is because while you trust their opinion, believe in them, care about their feelings, you do not really see yourself in them. Being in love makes judgment hazy—the endorphins flood your differences like a river delta and carry you both out to sea. But being near love, close but no cigar, means you get to see things closer to as they are because you see them differently than you would on your own. This is not unlike performance art, which asks you to take part in what you never forget is a performance. There is no script: only a happening in layers. Only then do you see the words.

The best times I had with the Performance Artist were the times I could let those happenings happen, when I was fine with the absence of any romantic future together and could simply enjoy the drive, near love like light is to dusk, so lovely as it fades into the night, the shimmery, sparkling conversation, as shimmery and real as "Did You See the Words" by Animal Collective, a song of layers and of meaning and of words writ on water.

Only Be Sure It Does Yield Fruit: A Playlist for Moments
Still in Motion

The Sundays, "Love"
Original creations—songs we make up
Broken Social Scene, "Ibi Dreams of Pavement"
Arcade Fire, "Here Comes the Night Time"

Sundays in Love: A Valentine

This is not about a lover at all. Instead, it is about one of the myriad associations stored up in memory, a link that seems weak and yet, in fact, makes me feel there is an ever-stronger web of joy netting me into this life through music.

When I think of the Sundays' 1992 song "Love," from their album *Blind*, I am anything but blind—so much fills my movie-picture mind. I think of my old best friend's best friend who I will call The Potter. So many layers of removal from intimacy there: I probably hung out with The Potter under ten times. I know he loved girls wearing sundresses and once made the most beautiful teapot in ceramics class—one with the face of Hermes on it. I know that now, he is happy, with many babies—more than he bargained for, in fact. The last "one" was triplets.

And that plentitude makes sense because what was always clear was that The Potter was a gentle soul, and he loved this song, would sing it lustily, particularly this line:

> *Well, if yoooooou*
> *don't have a clue about life*
> *then I'm happy, happy, happy to say*
> *neither have I*
> *although I'm not going to shrug my shoulders and*
> > *suck my thumb*
> *Thiiiis time*

Sometimes, people I adore move in and out of my life with a speed that both feeds and nauseates me—a form of emotional over-indulgence. In my non-music world, I'm a teacher, and after 30 years, I'm only now getting used to students bonding with me during their four years (or even just in their first year) and then disappearing into the ether after graduation, our closeness like a B-12 booster for their growth.

Of course, the opposite is true, too. I maintain many, many deep connections with many, many people.

But part of Valentine's Day for me, each year, is the time-lapse film of connections running through my head, of how many billions of loving Sundays I've felt. It can sometimes feel like a string of losses, sure. But—and this is what I love more—it can feel like the end of the movie *Cinema Paradiso*: a reel of all the good parts, spliced together, separate from their narratives but beautiful all alone. Snatches of verses, lines from a bridge, moments whose lovely tones make me think of lovely people I've known, their skillful tea pots, their warm-tea smile. I used to think of webs as fragile things in which we trap things. Now I think remembering even the friends of friends and what they loved is kind of like a web without a trap. Or maybe it's not a web at all. It's a kind of ceramic overglaze, fired over time, making something fragile seem solid, something in which we keep what we need.

I used to think I was the only one who made up songs for my cats. My tortoiseshell was greeted daily with this little kitty ditty: *"Judy / the Wonder Cat / not too tall and not too fat."* And one morning, with no intention of creation at all, I was inspired to compose on the spot, celebrating our differences: *"You are made of furrrrr / and I am made of skiiiiiiinnnnn / Your name is Judy, and my name, dear, is Bryn."*

Since then, I've written other hits, for other cats: "Nor Nor Superstar" (for my calico Nora) needs a stronger chorus, but I think I'm capturing something there about whether she is, in fact, a baby bunny or a cat. Arguably, the melody for "Luly Lu Lie" is plagiarized from The Kingsmen's "Louie Louie," but it seems no mere parody when Luly (my new tortoiseshell) races away from me to the open spaces of the living room. She clearly wants to dance.

I once had a guy write a song about me. He was really proud because, he said, "he got [my] eyes right." My eyes are brown. Here was the lyric: *Well, I think about your / dark brown eyes.*

Real love songs aren't always good because they're true or profound or even that original. They're good because you want to sing them, to tell another living creature your heart fills with music whenever they are near.

Whether they want to hear it or not[14].

---

[14] While Mark Kozelek of the Red House Painters is absolutely, completely, one of indie music's biggest, meanest, womanizing assholes, he does have a really, really beautiful song about his cat called "Wop-a-din-din." Check out my Spotify playlists for this book to hear it. Even Hitler loved his dog, I guess.

"I'm in love with a barback, and this is our song," I tell Xtina, over red wine on my white couch. The singer is Kishi Bashi, an electronic violinist, ethereal and epic; the song is "Q and A," with this chorus:

> *You are the answer to my question*
> *You are my accomplice in all crimes*
> *You are my wing woman and did I mention We were*
> *together in another life*
> *In that dreaming, you probably were my wife.*

I am in love again, and it is big. The best thing about falling in love after 40 is how much easier it is, how much less frightening, to contemplate realistically the future with the beloved, or, as my lover the Barback says, "The fear of asking big questions and giving big answers subsides with the realization that, when faced with something so good that so quickly becomes so necessary, it is NOT unreasonable to ask if it can be forever." He said that. Beautiful. True. Big. I am in love.

"But how did you decide it's your song?" asks Xtina. "Did you first kiss during it or cry during it or dance?" She tells me the story of her song. It was their first date, they were on the hill in Gasworks Park; Drew had brought his iPod and a plastic cup to amplify the sound. He played First Aid Kit's "Emmylou." She cried. He held her.

This is a good question, especially since I'd just told this new love, BB, two days before that our song is "Here Comes the Night Time" by Arcade Fire. "It HAS to be an Arcade Fire song," we agreed, for we would have never seen each other again, never known this love, if not for the two free tickets I had to the Gorge to see them. If not for the fact that no one could go with me, I would not have posted a last-minute offer on Facebook; if not for that offer, he would not have sat on his porch for two hours, wondering if he should write me, even though we hadn't seen each other in years; if not for that deliberation, his brother would not have told him, "What's the worst that could happen? Write her." If not for Facebook, this former student of mine from 2003 and 2004, when I was a grad student, would never have been in contact with me at all. Furthermore, if there had not been compassion in those years for a depressed freshman, he would not have contacted me at all, would not have saved, as he just realized this week, every paper he'd written for my class.

On a different set of "if nots," if not for Sam's betrayal of fi ve years ago[15], the breaking of m y own heart, he would not have sent me these tickets as a thank-you for forgiving him, for trying to return from lover to friend. That break-up, so awful I moved without telling him, sobbed a rib out of place . . . if not for that, I would not have the memory of standing on the observation deck of the Gorge with this new man in a summer twilight, golden as that entire day, as he told me about playing cello, and the whole world, that giant crowd, receded in the face of his face.

Does it, then, have to be Arcade Fire? But is "Here Comes the Night Time" the right song for our song? It *does* emphasize the uniqueness of that night, the sense of something big and epic and beautiful coming, of the importance of music in our relationship. *If there's no music in heaven, then what's it for?* So that song goes. It explores making choices against dogma; it reminds us *if you're looking for hell, just try looking inside.* So much of our conversation that night was about the power of reflection, how to work well with pain, instead of letting it make you bitter. So surely, this is our song, this finale, with its erratic rhythmic shifts, confetti canons, the Haitian drum breaks celebrating the other side of reflection, which is insight: *when you look at the sky, just try looking inside—God knows what you might find.* We were beside ourselves in that moment of the show—that is, we were the same.

Or is our song the simpler island song, "Haiti," during which these two relative strangers turned to each other and briefly slow danced, suddenly pulling away at the same moment, out of . . . what? We think nerves . . . or recognition. Is it the song during which I felt his arms around me from behind for the fi rst time, a spontaneous hug, as he shouted in my ear, "I am so glad you took me!!" We both remember this moment, the profound moment of contact. We don't remember which song, exactly, it was.

In his thank-you email to me the next day, subject line "I'm Still Feeling that Show!," the Barback New Love tells me he has been listening to "The Suburbs" again, the Arcade Fire's previous album. We have not yet told each other we are falling in love, and so he tells me, instead, how this concert was a needed gift, how "timing is everything," when it comes to understanding a song, how his new favorite song is "Ready to Start."

And we both are—ready to start this new creation, which feels

---

15 See "Divorce Closet."

like a whole album, a discography in the making, not just a single or even an EP.

"All art aspires to the condition of music," says my beloved Aesthete art critic and life guide, Walter Pater, for it is only in music that analysis fades away and we are left finally with the evocative, the "not-quite-yet-just-so." We are left with pure feeling, the sensation of something real beyond the Real we can articulate. That realness evolves, the more real we become to each other. Every day, I feel this as we love each other, and so, every day, we have a new song.

Dodging the Bullets, By Which I Mean Our Hearts

One year, I dodged a bullet and ran straight towards another; and then, I dodged that one, too. It was a strange love year, that year, and what I'll most remember about it is this sentence: "You dodged a bullet."

It's meant to be reassuring: a friend's arm around you, a deep sigh, as you're steered away from the scene of a great emotional crime or the hot mess of a person. The chorus of Broken Social Scene's "Ibi Dreams of Pavement" warns us against the hubris of taking on too much, the danger of engaging with others' grotesque failings: *And if God is what they made / cut their hands off, believers / Don't get high on what you create.* You end up on a couch with someone, recounting all the red flags: the smoking, the rehab, the silence about the future, the over-promising about the future, the annoying friends, any fact that didn't seem to want to touch you, etc. "I knew those things bothered me. I knew it from the start," you say, confused. And your friend pours you more red wine and pats your hand. "You don't have to care about those things anymore. You dodged a bullet."

But every time I hear that phrase, I feel bad, for a lot of reasons.

Because it puts me in a superior position, and that feels a little . . . superior. And does this bother me because I don't feel better than someone else or because I do?

I know I'm not a perfect partner: I don't make much money, if that's important to you. I'm a little helpless when it comes to technology and more than a little lazy. I always want every dead horse beaten to a pulp, by which I mean I can never let anything go. I make irritating generalizations about men. I have the occasional drunken outburst; at least twice, boyfriends have told me they don't enjoy pouring me into a car after weddings. But it's also true that my life has so few concrete "big" complications: no child, no lurking ex, a stable career and a job I love. My physical health is fine. I am emotionally happy, for the most part, and have been for years. No one's coming for me—creditors, former lovers, etc. But that's mostly just Doing Life and either not having made some of the Big Choices or having managed their consequences by this point in time. I hate writing this paragraph because it sounds like bragging. And maybe that's why my friends want to say it for me: "You dodged a bullet. That person doesn't have himself together. You do.

And you deserve better." I get that it's good to be met as an equal. Why do I still feel bad about asserting my own togetherness, much less the relatively high-functioning nature of that togetherness, as a standard by which I will search for others?

Because it makes me too aware of generic definitions of together-ness, and I hate the generic?

But "having yourself together" . . . there's got to be some mathematical term, some biological concept, for a series of evolving wholes. The Barback[16] told me his ex-girlfriend thought he had it together because he had a car, a child, a cool apartment, and was going back to school. "I told her, 'Yeah, but I'm just THIS CLOSE to it all collapsing, to not having it together,'" he said. Life, for him, was always just one step away from going on hold; it would take just one attack of his chronic illness to eradicate a new path. At least, that's what he felt. And I thought THAT was a red flag in and of itself: that he saw Life as a series of infinite dangers, that if one block crumbled, the whole wall would fall and there'd be no rebuilding. It was a red flag because this belief was predicated on another red flag: he had no faith that anyone would stick around to help him rebuild. He wouldn't let you. That is, he wouldn't let me. One unkind word from him, two unkind words from me. He claims I was the bullet. I claim he was the gun.

While I do like to think my form of togetherness has a sustainability, a resilience, I do understand how wholeness itself might be, at times, circumstantial, a fortuitous intersection of the right conditions with one's desires. The poststructuralist critics Deleuze and Guattari, in fact, saw the body itself as a fluid whole, ever becoming, a shifting series of plateaus (a "thousand," in their most famous work), rhizomes spreading out, forming subjectivities, plural. What could it mean to be "together," when one's own criteria for being (much less those of another, imposed upon one) change as we age?

What it could mean is that one is possibly both the target and the bullet.

Because when someone tells a woman she dodged a bullet, there's a kind of reinforcement that the smartest way to be in a relationship is to maintain a level of emotional safety, to choose only partners who won't require excessive care from you.

---

[16] See "When Our Song Became Just Mine" and "Aspiring to the Condition of Music: On Finding Your Song."

And that seems . . . like the worst version of the worst masculine stereotype.

I Googled "dodged a bullet," just to see what came up, and it was pretty awful, but it was mostly pretty awful because it seemed like there were a lot of links for men about "crazy women" and how a guy could know whether he'd dodged a bullet. I won't provide links to these. They were callous, and they were cruel, but the overall tenor of them was this: you dodged a bullet if she's "making a big deal" out of some-thing--the relationship, the break-up, etc. "Making a big deal," "causing drama" . . . all these seemed like euphemisms for "caring," to me. But instead of "caring," the word these sites used was this: "insecure."

If you've read the rest of this book, this conflation of vul-nerability with insecurity might sound familiar. And it does still anger me—not, I feel certain, because I am "insecure" but because he judged my admission of vulnerability from a place of distance, when he had been requiring that his own admissions be met with love. His vulnera-bility was "self- aware" and "rational"; mine was "insecure" and "dark." Leslie Jamison's beautiful essay "In Defense of Saccharin(e)" considers the myriad ways we in academia are taught to avoid excess, to refine our feelings and thinking while rejecting refined sugar in any form, aesthetic or otherwise, as if, in doing so, we can prove our superiority to feeling. We want to believe, says Jamison, we're better than simple emotions leading us to clear-cut disasters of feeling, smart enough to know what feelings are worth it and which are not:

We dispatch entire works, entire genres in the clean guillotine strokes of these words: saccharine, syrupy, sentimental. It's as if sentimen-tality is something we don't need to define. We only need to hate it, shield ourselves from it, articulate ourselves against it—thus assert-ing that we are arbiters of artistry and subtlety, an elite so sensitive we don't need the same forceful quantities of feeling. We will subsist more delicately, we say. We will subsist on less. In this, we make sure we're not mistaken for the rest of the world, whose sensibilities are too easily moved by crude surfaces of feeling or meaning. We don't examine the contours of sentimentality; we simply eschew them. We don't worry about the fine line between melodrama and pathos, we simply assert that we're camped on the proper side of the divide.

In one strand of the essay, a younger Jamison eschews "girly drinks" for whiskey, a strategy to look tougher, smarter—to look, frankly, "male." It is a strategy of which I am guilty—as if whiskey will inoculate me against the bullet I'm clearly courting, a way to have my deep feelings and still seem "securely" invulnerable from them.

Near the end of Broken Social Scene's "Ibi Dreams of Pavement," the lyrics link "dodging a bullet" to not only vulnerability but to love and, particularly, women's love:

> *And if love is what they gave, Turn*
> *wives into healers*
> *Don't get high on what you create Or it*
> *might just steal ya*

Excessive caring is "feminine." Looking out for yourself and not caring are "masculine." And the gendering of it all—of avoiding those who will "cause drama" or who aren't as "together" as we are, the cautioning against a wife becoming healer . . . it makes me think that what troubles me most about the phrase "dodging a bullet" is that it encourages us all to think of caring about those who need care as involving oneself in an act of danger, an obliteration of the individual self.

Which, in fact, it is. Or, at the least, isn't there is an alteration of the self because it has put itself in the way of vulnerability, in the path of something fast moving and vital?
But isn't all vulnerability a risk? And don't we cringe at that cliché because we want to believe someday, we will understand fully all the warning signs in advance and do everything just right, as if the signs don't change as often as what counts as danger for us as we grow, our thousand plateaus shifting?

I know that there are risks and RISKS. I don't want to take care of someone who won't take care of me. I don't want to be with someone I cherish but who won't mirror back the courage I try to have when I stand in the way, willingly, of what makes them crumble. I don't want someone who will not sweetly, graciously catch me when someday I also fall. A yoga teacher used to end class by encouraging us to "protect your heart with wisdom—give your heart with courage." I've thought a lot about the first part of this . . . but isn't it painful to think of so many people as bullets, of ourselves in need of so much protection, as if giving weren't, itself, eventually to be the result?

Don't I carry within the barrel of my own heart, a bullet I hope, someday, someone won't dodge?

160

EP

Emotional Discography: A Lonely Year in Three Albums
   Angel Olsen, *Burn Your Fire for No Witness*
   Other Lives, *Rituals*
   Car Seat Headrest, *Teens of Style*

Emotional Discography: A Lonely Year in Three Albums

Part I: Angel Olsen--Burn Your Fire for No Witness

> *I quit my dreaming the moment that I found you I started*
> *dancing just to be around you*
> *Here's to thinking that it all meant so much more I kept*
> *my mouth shut and opened up the door I wanted nothing*
> *but for this to be the end*
> *For this to never be a tied and empty hand*
> *If all the trouble in my heart would only end I lost my*
> *dream, I lost my reason all again*
> *It's not just me for you*
> *I have to look out too*
> *I have to save my life*
> *I need some peace of mind*
> *I am the only one now*
> *You may not be around*

I fi rst heard Angel Olsen's "Forgiven/Forgotten" and bought the album without realizing that song was by far the most optimistic on the whole thing. "Forgiven / Forgotten" is about two minutes long and the cheerful theme song for one of my longest-standing problems: a tendency to continue to take emotional risks, even when it's been established that there will be no pay-off.

In *The Anniversary Party,* Kevin Kline and his five-year-old daughter reenact the rocky marriage of the couple (Alan Cumming and Jennifer Jason Leigh) whose anniversary it is: at one point, he pushes her dramatically away from him; she walks sadly away, only to turn and rush back, to fling herself back into his only partially extended arms. I cry every time, identifying with the five-year-old. "Forgiven/Forgotten" went on the last CD I made for my camp romance, which began when I was 16 and ended, oh, when I was 41. It was a torch carried, primarily, by me, but surely fueled, in part, by his alcoholism, that most useful of fuels for oblivion and denial. The CD was part of a last-ditch attempt to forgive someone who didn't think he'd done anything wrong, who wanted, moreover, to be forgotten.

Why did I do it? In "Dance Slow Decades," Angel Olsen seemed to know: *I dance because I know this one.*

More recently, I tried to explain a questionable romantic entanglement to a dear friend and her husband. "I mean, who's it going to hurt, other than myself?" I said. They looked first at each other, then at me, and said, "Exactly, honey."

But the rest of the album isn't about that—it isn't about self-destruction, about flinging oneself at all. It's not about risk as much as it is accountability: that quality most essential to a risk, without which a "risk" is merely carelessness. It's an album about facing loneliness and choosing to be oneself. *If you've still got some light in you, then go before it's gone / Burn your fire for no witness / it's the only way it's done*, Olsen sings in "White Fire." Lindsay Zoladz agrees in her *Pitchfork* review of the album:

> *"Hi-Five", the third song on Angel Olsen's second album, Burn Your Fire for No Witness, has got to be one of the most cheerful songs ever written about being lonely. [. . .] "Are you lonely too?" Olsen warbles. A beat later, her band's back in full Technicolor, and the next line hits like a title card in an old Batman episode: "HI-FIVE! / SO AM I!"*

When 2015 began, I was still recovering from yet another brutal break-up with The Barback, and I found a new theme song: "Unfuck the World," quoted at the beginning of this section. It's the first song on the album, and it sounds like the kind of song a sad girl would write alone in her bedroom. Since I *was* a sad girl writing alone in my bedroom, I curled into it like a cat curls into a small space when it's feeling insecure.

I was suffering to a degree clearly disproportionate to the relationship, feeling an anger I sensed was not about The Barback. And when I heard this song, I knew why. I really did love him, but I also loved that he seemed ready to give me everything I had wanted . . . with Elliott, the boyfriend before him. Once, in the first month of our three months together, I'd mentioned that even after three years, Elliott was never comfortable talking about getting married. The Barback turned to me. "How long do you think is rational before we move in together and get engaged?" I looked up at him, startled. "Two or three years?" I said, weakly. "Well, I'm thinking six months to a year," he responded. "Elliott didn't know what he had." Maybe he didn't, and maybe the Barback didn't either, or maybe I'm just that good at inciting the one unpleasant confrontation that will end even the most committed of relationships. But Angel Olsen knew—she knew what I had. *I lost my dream, I lost my reason all again.*

My heart wasn't just breaking—it was rebroken, in all the most sensitive places. My grief over the end of my relationship with Elliott had only reached the bargaining stage by the time I met the Barback, and I saw him, his readiness to talk about big things with me, to actively love me enough to want a future with me, as part of the bargain: maybe if I just make the strong choice, maybe if I break up with Elliott even though I love him, I will still find a lover who chooses me without hesitation and get what I want. *I wanted nothing but for this to be the end.*

And that awareness unleashed the next phase of grieving: anger. It's the emotion your friends least want to hear about, the emotion you least want to feel towards someone you once loved most. But what I learned about anger over the first five months of this last year was that it is a motivator. In "Enemy," Olsen gently confronts her own disillusionment and comes to terms with the tricks her own mind has played on her:

> *I wish it were the same*
> *as it is in my mind*
> *I am lighter on my feet*
> *when I've left some things behind*

I knew (and still know) the anger I felt was less about either man and more about having to force myself to move forward to face being alone—really, really alone.

And I hate it. I still hate it, mostly. I enjoy my own company, and I do meaningful things, but I am an extrovert, and it's just not as much fun for me to have as much alone time as I do. This essay isn't going to end with me finding out how much I love being alone. The anger has dissipated somewhat, but it's still there sometimes, although it's changed directions. (Why can't I better appreciate what so many wish they could have—this intimate time with oneself?) I still know I would far rather have a partner than be singing soft songs to myself in my bedroom. But this album repeated to me, again and again, the soft song that would be more useful to sing:

> *It's not just me for you*
> *I have to look out too*
> *I have to save my life*
> *I need some peace of mind*

I am the only one now I am the only
one now I am the only one now You
may not be around You may not be
around You may not be around

You'd think this would have been obvious—we all die in our
own arms, anyway. But somehow, this was the year in which I understood that I might not have someone there near the end and that I might
want to start getting used to that idea. I don't like it. But this awareness
feels meaningful. Again, the *Pitchfork* review offers me a way to think
about this meaning and grow:

> *Olsen knows too well that dreamers are usually loners. Not that she really*
> *minds. If she seems unafraid of—even superhumanly amped about—*
> *loneliness, it's because her songs find an almost beatific peace in solitude. "If*
> *you can't be psyched about your own thoughts," she said in an interview a few*
> *years ago, "Then how are you supposed to have a meaningful interaction with*
> *anyone?"*

I'm in the process of growing right now, of trying both to be open to
emotions as they come, without turning them into dreamy narratives,
and to stand up for myself and what feels useful, if not good. If this
year began with track one of Burn Your Fire for No Witness, it seems
apt that it has ended with me thinking more about the final track,
"Windows." After a whole album of confronting oneself and others,
Olsen reminds me that all the confrontation is not just for the sake of
self-awareness—it's so we can feel better. I spent a lot of time alone
with my thoughts last year, and some of them were powerful. The
meaningful interactions were there, too. And I hope I can keep feeling
better.

> *We throw our shadows down*
> *we must throw our shadows down we live and*
> *throw our shadows down it's how we get around*
> *What's so wrong with the light?*

Other Lives is not a band I listen to for lyrics, which says a lot, considering I'm a Word Girl. Thus, in a year when I felt more inward, more silent, it makes sense that their album *Rituals* filled that silence with its own quiet movement. I saw them twice last year, once at the free concerts on the lawn of Seattle Center's Mural Amphitheater but once, more importantly, on a Tuesday night, in the dark, packed night club Neumo's, by myself. In her review of *Rituals*, their second album, music critic Kelsey Simpkins describes going to an Other Lives show herself: "The music rolled through our bodies, beat our hearts for us." After the first third of the year, the survival of a break-up, the sadness of deep loneliness, Other Lives ushered me into a different room in the house of myself and beat my heart for me, asking me only to be there.

> *Come live on in silence,*
> *Everything's standing out like a loss and feels like*
>   *I've been*
> *I won't fear my babbles*
> *leave them in the silence*
> *I live in the present*
> *moment to moment*

"Reconfiguration" is a ghost call of a song, taking part of its power from one member of the band doing a strange imitation of what seems like a child playing "Indian," fluttering his hand over his voice to make a sound both eerie and owl-like. The album itself was a reconfiguration for me: of loneliness into, for a time, merely solitude. Emily Dickinson says "One need not be a chamber to be haunted," but for much of the spring and summer, I was only a chamber, a space I was uncertain how to fill. I was, finally, un-haunted, true: mostly busy with work, focused on writing, coming to terms with the dark angers of the winter. I returned to my writing, talking more and more to myself, writing so much that, at times, I felt I'd replaced actual intimacy with these revisitings of my own losses, the babbles of my own heart. Simpkins also describes the album as "a series of smaller, detailed listening experiences," and each essay I wrote seemed, to me, like a tiny desk concert, a pleasure best experienced alone.

Moreover, Other Lives is the kind of show you can go to see by yourself and never feel alone. Usually, when a band plays for its audience, for me, there are these moments of feeling more, not less, separate from them: they talk to the audience and make jokes; the audience laughs, and the people around you nudge each other knowingly or comment on what's just been said. In contrast, it doesn't seem to me that Other Lives plays for the audience, really—they play for themselves, for each other. Attention isn't called to the fact that you have no one to nudge, no one with whom to comment, because attention stays on the music, orchestral, multi-layered, unfolding before you like a thunderstorm coming across the empty Oklahoman plains from which the band itself comes, and the only thing to do is smell the ozone in the air and close your eyes as the first warm drops hit your upturned face, softly at first, until your skin gives over and becomes part of what the rain comes to fill.

I've always felt like that—like their music is a coming storm; I was unsurprised, then, to find the image used by Simpkins:

Like dynamic paint strokes, intimate choreography, and electrifying storms, Rituals evokes the aesthetic experience of life itself in its finest moments. The opening track, "Fair Weather," is the like the gathering of a rainstorm from a long time coming. And Rituals is that rainstorm: spilling its long-accumulated contents on us in a deluge. [T]here is a sound of uprooting, of displacement in Rituals, both physical and mental; an unsettling feeling of change since the release of Tamer Animals, and an attempt to redefine oneself anew.

Perhaps, as a former Kansan, I still feel that displacement, understand how the "attempt to redefine oneself anew" will always recall not just the meek and constant rain of the Northwest but the electrical anticipation of the thunderstorms of the Midwest. Perhaps that is why it was such a surprise to find myself beginning to settle into the solitude, and why I still fight against that feeling, at times. Change, for me, has always been charged—coming from a place I did not love, looking for things I could not find easily, I have long been unfamiliar with the feeling of life simply moving on. More often, I have placed myself in the way of the deluge, daring myself to be uprooted: leaving Seattle, a city I loved, for a tenure-track job in a tiny town in Missouri, returning to Seattle, accepting the spontaneous moment, inviting others to do so, in return, turning over the unturned stones to see if glass hearts were buried underneath, throwing my own glass heart at hard surfaces to see how strong it is, to find out what it means, exactly, when glass breaks.

Yet last year was a year in which change did not have charge. Spring quarter came and went; summer began. I wrote in spring. I read in spring. I read what my students wrote in spring, and in summer, I wrote and read what I wrote, again and again, trying to figure out not how to change my life next but how to reorganize what has happened in it. I saw Other Lives again, at the Mural, on a lawn with a hundred other people and my friend Leah. But still, I loved them more that time I saw them alone, when I was simply in the process of living. "In their element," Simpkins says, "[lead singer Jessie] Tabbish's lyrics come effortlessly, like in a dream, and the sounds feel like they've always existed."

And that is why their song "Patterns" is my favorite song on the album. Although I did not know the lyrics at the time, it is as if I had understood all along, had heard the ironic tension in the song between immersion in the moments of the present and the realization that one is repeating, again, those same moments which have led your heart astray before, experiencing as new those emotional changes in tempo and dynamic, which are, in fact, not changes at all:

> Put yourself first, and feel yourself, and then I
> wander in sleep, in a silent tone.
> Put yourself far, and feel yourself in mine, I'm
> wandering still, falling in love so far
> Into your arms, into the void
> Oh I should have known.
> Oh I should have known better.

But the musical patterns in the song itself are so lovely, so lacey, so intricate, shimmering starlight across the deeper wells of an ocean, that you don't experience the repetition as such—much as I'd begun to find the return of the same placid day less of a disappointment because it brought no change. Simpkins quotes Tabbish, saying *Rituals* "'was about the spontaneity of travel and being isolated. For the first times in our lives we were moving off on our own away from our families and kind of coming into our own.'" For me, *Rituals* played on repeat-all in my chamber as I moved constantly while standing still, as I moved away from one version of loneliness to be, more firmly, in the same place. Or so it seemed.

But remember—there I was: simply letting their music beat my heart for me, standing alone near the stage, closing my eyes and letting the music itself be what I felt, while lyrics like this were sung to me, whispering into me like the temperature of the rain which you notice, primarily, for its pressure:

> The more that you give, the
> less that you fear the less that
> you fear

"The vision of *Rituals*," Simpkins' review ends, "needs the time to communicate its story." Perhaps my own vision does, too—time to be lonely, alone, silent, while the patterns emerge and change me, rain on the sand.

Part III: Car Seat Headrest, Teens of Style—Why 42 is the New 24

I should be too old for this album.

But I was in the car, on my way to Ballard in October, and I heard this song on its tin-can-line to my soul, the lo-fi production exactly the right timbre for the low-grade discontent creeping around in my life, just like this bass line lurks around the corners of this song. And the repetitive, somewhat abrasive synth riff was the bright light in the middle, shaking me out of that driver's spell, and asking me to listen and to care. And some boy-man was singing, with that kind of resignation 400 yards away from actually feeling bad, *Maud / now you're gone / now you're gah ah ah ah ah ah ah ahn.*

The song was "Maud Gone," a play on Yeats's fierce Maud Gonne, the band (really just a singer) was Car Seat Headrest, and the album, I would find, was *Teens of Style*.

Teens of Style. Teens.

It might be classic to say "I'm too old for this," but this is my first mid-life crisis. So, it's new for me to say it.

Will Toledo, of Car Seat Headrest, is actually 23. Will Toledo is a year out of college. Will Toledo was just signed by Matador Records, the label of Pavement and Modest Mouse—bands actually my own age. Will Toledo sings lyrics like this: *I can't talk to my folks and I want to kick my dad in the shins.*

My dad is dead. I've been out of college 22 years, almost as long as Will Toledo's been alive. I find those lyrics painfully young. But too old or not, I love this album. I love it. And I think it's because it helps me see why 42 is the new 24.

Here's why. Collin Brennan's article "Why Car Seat Headrest is the Indie Hero We've Been Waiting For" has a subheading, and it's this:

"Will Toledo isn't perfect. But he's loud, honest, and painfully aware of his place in the world." Check. Check, check, and check. Isn't that basically the description of a midlife crisis?

I have two things to tell you about loneliness. No. Three.

Heavy Boots on My Throat / I Need Something Soon

"Something Soon" is a song about the anxiety of not knowing what you want next but knowing that something needs to happen. I've been in that place for about, oh, two or three years. Perhaps that's why I write about the past so much. In the face of anxieties about my career (the dean wanted to cut my position three weeks ago. It's safe. For now), the possibilities I'm letting go of (marriage, children, home ownership), and the patterns I'm coming to accept (what if it really IS just me forever? What if I always AM going to be this lazy?), I find it immensely comforting to take what's already happened and mine it for the insight and intimacy I have difficulty accessing as of late. Or, as Will Toledo puts it, *I was referring to the present in past tense / It was the only way that I could survive it.*

SO GOOD.

> *The other lyrics are, quite simply, a list of Wants and Needs: I want to*
> *break something important*
> *I want to kick my dad in the shins*
> *[. . . .]*
> *I want to close my head in the car door*
> *I want to sing this song like I'm dying*
> *Heavy boots on my throat I need*
> *I need something soon*
> *I need something soon*
> *I can't talk to my folks I need*
> *I need something soon*
> *I need something soon*
> *All of my fingers are froze I need*
> *I need something soon*
> *I need something soon*
> *Only one change of clothes I need*
> *I need something soon*
> *I need something soon*

Oh, but the heavy boots are so different now, at 42. It's not so much the pressure from others but your own boots on your own throat. It's not that, at 24, you aren't hard on yourself, but from what I remember, you have that sense that somehow, you'll be shown the right way, if only you can find the right something.

But that's its own problem: I have so many right somethings. They crowd each other and jockey for space; they whisper unkind things about each other from opposite corners in my head. In one of my favorite moments in "Something Soon," Will Toledo talks over himself:

> *I want to talk like Raymond Carver (an*
> *advertisement cries out)*
> *I want to turn down the goddamn TV ("He*
> *should have gone to Jared's")*

I tell myself I'm not lazy—I did plenty of worthy things this week. ("Yes," my mind says, "but you also binge-watched *The Miss Fisher Murder Mysteries* for four hours and drove to yoga, instead of walking.") I like how honest I am as a teacher. ("But your evaluations are always split—you need to change somehow." "But how?" "If you stopped being so lazy, you'd figure that out. This is why your job is insecure. Maybe you should leave your job entirely. Lord.")

Ok, so maybe it's not so much that there are so many "right things" but rather that there are a lot of opposing tendencies within me: to accept myself as close to completely as I can while staying, like Will Toledo, "painfully aware of [my] place in the world."

There's a Full Moon Every Night / It's Just Not Always Bright

I heard "Maud Gone," still my favorite song on *Teens of Style*, in the autumn. Autumn is the best teaching quarter, any teacher will tell you: you are convinced you're going to be better, the students come back, convinced they're going to be better. I had great classes. Professionally, things seemed good. But I was about 500 yards away from my heart, which is why I love the tinny detachment and simultaneous hopefulness of this song.

It accepts that maybe something is gone (Maud, in this case), but it has enough distance to wonder "when did our heart stop beating?" It also wonders how to get a grip on the heavy boots from before—in my case, the sense that a fulfilling career isn't in bed with you at night, which can turn any reflection into a more existential problem:

172

When I'm in bed
I'm dead
No one to check my pulse
And so instead
My head
Begs not to be so full
and when I fall
asleep
which part of me writes the dream
and which part falls
asleep
who's running the machine?
But it also suggests maybe you need to try some thing
different:
I know there's a full moon every night
it's just not always bright
but it's been so long since I saw the light
maybe I haven't been looking at the sky

So I did. I looked at the sky, forgetting something Will Toledo says in another song: *I hadn't looked at the sun for so long / I'd forgotten how much it hurts to*. I had an affair—a dark, intense, raw release from my head into my body. He was so different from me that, at first, I found myself quivering in what might have been a romance novel cliché, if it didn't feel so bad. But soon, I felt hyper-sensitive to his criticisms, which seemed strangely almost like compliments. Everything he liked about me also seemed to be something that drove him crazy: "You've got this bubble around you," he told me once, "that's almost . . . fairy-like? And usually, my instinct with that is to try to poke holes in it. But I can't fi nd any holes with you. I guess that's who you really are."

He was driven, fierce, strong, dark, masculine, and hot as fuck-ing hell. He was a Scorpio. Does that help? Or excuse the fact that I was scared of him? It helped me—to know exactly why this bad moon was so diffi cult but also why it kept a-risin.' Once, in February, we were buried in each other at the corner table of Tini Bigg's, a martini bar known for its dark corners for dark people. The waitress came over and mentioned she remembered us . . . from November. "Probably because we couldn't stop groping each other, which makes it hard to take a drink order," he muttered in my ear, as she walked away, and our hands moved towards each other under the table.

But Scorpio was not my boyfriend, which is where the tinny detachment comes in. He was a lover, and he was not mine. Still, he eclipsed all others and I could see no other moons, full and bright or otherwise. I would watch him walk out my front door, after an afternoon in bed, always going back to his other world. And when he was gone, I would wonder whether it was worth it. But I was also forced to consider whether I needed a partner and how much of one I really needed. I investigated whether intensity itself could be enough, what my real boundaries were. He pulled my heart out of my chest and made me look at it again, and he made it beat. Hard. In short, he denied me the bridge:

> *Sweetheart please love me too long My*
> *heart's too strong*
> *Love me too long*
> *Sweetheart please let me hold on To these*
> *old songs*
> *I've loved too long*

And whether you're 24 or 42, you need to know when to learn new songs. There is such a thing as holding on just because you're used to something being there: like old songs, old ideas about what you want, old patterns, old ghosts. Like the moon.

You Have No Right to be Depressed / You Haven't Tried Hard Enough to Like It

I read this morning that whereas the Baby Boomer midlife crisis was about rejecting convention, the *Mad Men* life they thought they should want, the Generation Xer's midlife crisis is about agoraphobia: instead of shrinking opportunities, there are still so many. And because I haven't taken up some of the traditional ones (marriage-baby-house-dog), I can see why some might think I am the author of my own crisis, the author now of so many narratives of loneliness and loss. After the Angel Olsen essay, an acquaintance who has never lived alone in her adult life told me, self-righteously, "It sounds like you just really need to learn how to love yourself."

I want her to listen to Millennial Will Toledo's new song, "Fill in the Blank." You know what he's so tired of, he tells us? *Fill in the blank.* You know what kind of answer he gets when he says this? *You have no right to be depressed / you haven't tried hard enough to like it.* Will Toledo finds that answer, as do I, infuriating. But he tries to engage with that cliché and acknowledges that, yes, he may not have *seen enough of this world yet / But it hurts, it hurts, it hurts, it hurts.* I want to quote Brennan at length here because Will Toledo and I both get what you, Judgmental Friend, are saying about taking ownership over your own life, and we want you to know that we mean it, too, when we are ambiv-alent about that ownership:

> *Lots of folks would take one look at Toledo and be quick to write him off as a hipster. The songs don't always help his case in this regard, stuffed as they are with irony and wry cynicism. But any-one who sits down with Car Seat Headrest for a while comes to find that one of the band's dominant traits is earnestness. Even the ideas that seem silly on the surface (ahem, "Drunk Drivers/Killer Whales") end up as rousing, tear-jerking anthems that tug on all the right heartstrings. This is perhaps the most important — and least talked about — aspect of great rock music: the sentimentality that flirts with cheesiness, the absolute conviction that a song can change the world, or at least somebody's world, for even just a little while. Teens of Denial, on its surface, is the product of a proto-typical millennial mindset. You have no right to be depressed/ You haven't tried hard enough to like it, Toledo sings on opener "Fill in the Blank," a song whose lyrics practically overflow with snark. But undermining those lyrics is a rock beat that straight-up grooves and a squealing guitar melody that wants to be heard over an arena's loudspeakers.*

I love myself plenty. I'm just trying to answer the ultimate Talking Heads question—"How did I get here?"—without the beautiful house, the beautiful wife. Sometimes, without those markers, it's harder to understand what kind of life you're authoring or at least for other people to understand. I mostly think this IS my beautiful life.

So, thank you, Will Toledo, for reminding me that wondering aloud about these questions is ok: "I think part of being an artist is remaining vulnerable to human opinion," he reflects in Brennan's piece. "You always want to hide away the immaturity with yourself, and I guess for me this is a way of refusing myself that luxury."

This is me refusing myself that luxury. My year was about con-frontations and some self-indulgent immaturity and some new maturity and listening to Car Seat Headrest sigh and mumble and scream *you guys got mad skillz / I just got mad.* And it was boring and peaceful and angry and productive and weird and dark and, sometimes, really, really FUN. Just like *Teens of Style*.

Car Seat Headrest's new album comes out in two days: *Teens of Denial.* I don't think either Will Toledo or I are in denial about much anymore.

Burning, the Remix

Conclusion

     Sharon Van Etten, "Jupiter 4"

"Hardly Time to Make Theories": Some Reflections on Writing about Music and Intimacy or, Pandora for the Emotions

"I was dreaming when I wrote this / forgive me if it goes astray."
—Prince

What the Academic Abstract Would Look Like: Pater's Nightmare

This conclusion reflects on changes in my initial anxieties but also on what I've found about how we all use music and what it shows about us. Some of these insights may be common sense: music can cause feelings to linger or change, we often use music to communicate what we cannot. But other insights are more culturally revealing: the ways in which men and women use music in relation to emotions is often quite different, people will treat you like they treat their music. In the end, this conclusion shows I have some strategies for understanding my heart but that, as I will always remember from Pater, those strategies must always remain in flux, responsive to the moment, and that the moment will always be fueled with music.

What I Really Feel: The Burning

I was ten years younger when I wrote the introduction to this book. Did I learn strategies for understanding my heart?

Instead of a list of lessons learned, I want to play you my final impressions on shuffle. For, as my beloved Pater says, "With this sense of the splendor of our experience and of its awful brevity, gathering all we are into one desperate effort to see and touch, we shall hardly have time to make theories about the things we see and touch. What we have to do is to be forever curiously testing new opinions and courting new impressions, never acquiescing in a facile orthodoxy . . . ." Burn the abstract.

That said, let's dance:

> **Music can supplant intimacy, and this can happen because I am a sucker for music used as a way to my heart. But, if the final The Quiet One had been into Metallica (sorry—just not my band), I doubt that I would have tricked myself so thoroughly into believing what we shared was love.*

179

*Most often, though, music augments intimacy. Love songs are truer, sad songs are sadder, and lyrics are more meaning-ful when they echo what we already believe and feel. Despite all the negative things to be said about the Red-Headed Architect, that moment in Rome when we split an iPod would still have existed and we would have been close . . . but beyond that, the song itself is now a web for me, hold-ing together all the visceral elements in that moment: the temperature of the air, the sounds outside on the Campo, the pressure of his hand are all brought back in the tone of that song.

*Music can provide us with a way into and out of a relation-ship. Knowing that The Painter loved the song "There Goes the Fear" helped me understand how desperately he want-ed to overcome his own fears; it moved me towards him. "Fleurette Africaine" articulated the melancholy that ran, like a silent stream, beneath the always troubled relationship with The Quiet One, and helped me know that there was only one ending for us.

*Women seem to use music as background for other aspects of intimacy; men seem to use it as foreground. Songs were keys to larger maps for Cara, and the terrain itself for the Performance Artist.

*People will treat you like they treat their music. Multiple mixed CDs can either mean they have that much to say and share with you, or that they are endlessly deflecting attention from who they are to what they want you to think they are. And after a while, too many mixes focused only on the most contemporary music start to feel like running on disappear-ing ground, instead of establishing something on which to stand. This is an observation full of holes. I'm still thinking about whether this is true. I do think that people who are always looking for the Japanese import EP with rare B sides are going to ditch you faster. But I also don't like being with people who think music ended with the Beatles broke up. The former are obsessed with the ephemeral, while the *latter are too blindly loyal. All I'm saying is I like to see some range in what someone offers me, some Aretha Franklin alongside some Billie Eilish. It shows me your world con-tains multitudes.*

*The hardest part of organizing a book about music is figuring out the order of the playlists. I so didn't want this book to move from break-ups to perfect healing. So many essays are out of actual chronological order, in terms of when they happened. Love moves like grief, you see, which is to say, it follows no order.

*I have loved easily and often. I am so glad.

**Forgiveness is easy if you really trusted the person before the wound because trust isn't actually easily broken. What's easily broken are illusions of trust, which are what you
wanted to believe and didn't share with another.*

*Music can give you access to illusory things you still want to believe and do share with another, like deals with God or slow dances that continue even when the music's ended or folk songs you still know all the words to and hope to sing again.

*Always, always there is music. And there will always, always be more of it.

This project took me years, and there was a point at which I stopped writing these essays. I hadn't even run out of people or songs. I wanted to write about the tape my best male friend in college made me with snippets of our favorite movie, *L.A. Story*, recorded from television, in between songs. I wanted to write about how my gentle mother would terrify four-year-old me when she'd play Berlioz's "Dream of a Witches' Sabbath" or "March to the Scaffold" or the 4th movement from *Symphonie Fantastique*, and how it both thrilled and scared me again to hear it in the Julia Roberts movie Sleeping with the Enemy.

But *something* felt finished. "I feel different," I told my friend Brandi[17], who'd read every essay. "Do I seem different?" "You talk

---

[17] See "What is the Light," radiation mixes section.

about the past less," she said and squeezed my hand.

Maybe it wasn't "finished" I felt, but *full*. Not necessarily perfect or always happy, but full. Of course, many think of writing as a purging, a way to air the wounds and clean them. Eliza Smith's "The Wound and the Essayist" quotes essayist Chelsea Biondolillo, who "recognizes wound-holding as an allowance of the form, rather than a prerequisite: 'The wound needs to be protected, these essays seem to imply, with something hard and calcareous. Something spiny, perhaps, or even pearled. Something you might want to pick up, even if it is chipped.'" That is, writing about hard stuff gives you a way not to cut your hand while you find the pearl. I'd aged into a time of life when dating wasn't quite as much fun, though there was still fun to be had, burning left to do. But while there were shells aplenty (Scorpios, I wasn't sure about the pearls. The quality of my experiences had changed, the tone of the exploration. It was like I'd listened to everything in the store: Doves could still make me cry, but I didn't wonder why so much anymore.

But here is the surprising thing: that lack of wonder didn't feel so bad. I'd become, somehow, a writer—not wanting to look back so much, not needing to burn so brightly for anyone else. I wanted more to read and write and hear the words today—to talk to others about rolling their hearts up into velvet or how to cut the gem of their pain, how to facet life in sparkle. To love the gems of my life as they were, instead of diving back into raw experiences, looking for pearls.

I was wearing a sequined flapper dress when I met The Stage Craft Technician at Elena's[18] Christmas party. Wait—no more pseudonyms. No more. No more reason to protect the innocent, the guilty, whatever that might mean. I met Rick.

Sitting on a couch, we'd spoken of many things: teaching, how much we liked Manhattans, Bizarro's, a restaurant I loved owned by his friend, and then I brought up music. "I *love* Car Seat Headrest," I said. Rick's eyes turned liquid with what looked very near love. "Same," he said.

The last to leave the party, we agreed to go to dinner at Bizarro's after I returned from Christmas break in ten days. I was leaving Wednesday. We hugged. *Maybe I misread that guy—maybe he just wants to be friends,* I thought. Arriving home at 1:00 a.m., I texted "It was so nice to meet you." "Same" flashed back, and we texted for an hour, until our phones ran low on battery. Maybe I didn't misread him, and I am certain

---

[18] See "What Is the Light," radiation mixes section.

we smile, sometimes, when we sleep.

Sunday, I awoke to find a picture from him of coffee and *East of Eden* by Steinbeck, turned to page one—I'd said it was a favorite of mine. By midday, another text: "Can you go out before you leave?" A Monday date, and by the time my plane touched down in Kansas Wednesday, we'd had our first kiss, sent three hours' worth of songs back and forth over the phone. Dinner at Bizarro's on my return, New Year's Eve, meeting up "just for one drink" and staying out for hours on work nights, loathe to leave each other. Two months later during a snowstorm, he moved in, and we listened all the way through to Sharon Van Etten's album *Remind Me Tomorrow*, tears on both our faces. It didn't remind me of tomorrow—it felt completely like today.

"All art aspires to the condition of music," it's true. But maybe all writing about music aspires, finally to more love: to know how you love, how to listen better, to find out what's come before, to recognize a remix of old stuff that just changes the beat, to celebrate what's new. All those things are present in what we call our song; it's from that same Sharon Van Etten album, a song with the mysterious title "Jupiter 4." We looked it up, and it's just a kind of synthesizer. It's the sound that she was after, but the lyrics anyway that make it ours. They feel so private, we don't know if we can bear to play it at our wedding in July. So, I will play it for you now and leave you with music—that is, leave you with love:

> *Our love's for real*
> *How'd it take a long, long time*
> *To let us feel*
> *Try to relate in my state*
> *And the aura around me says*
> *My love is for real*
> *Touching your face*
> *How'd it take a long, long time*
> *To be here*
> *Turning the wheel on my street*
> *My heart still skips a beat*
> *It's echoing, echoing, echoing, echoing,*
> *echoing, echoing*
> *Baby, baby, baby*

I've been searching for you
I want to be in love
Baby, baby, baby
I've been waiting, waiting,
*   waiting my whole life*
For someone like you
It's true that everyone would like to have met A love
so real
A love so real

Acknowledgements

While thanking Facebook is questionable, this book only exists because of my many Facebook friends who read the seeds of these essays when they were just baby posts and who encouraged me to develop them. You have no idea what it meant to tell me you were waiting for the next one, and you all turned me into a writer. Thank you for every "like," and I love you.

Thank you to Otherwords Press and my editor Kate Benson, who asked to see my whole manuscript after accepting the Devo essay. You are evidence in this world that sometimes, people really just want to help you. Also, taxidermy is cool.

Sonora Jha, Juan Reyes, and Susan Meyers, thank you also for taking my writing seriously and giving me space in our workplace to be one. And thanks also to those colleagues who knew this was more than just "professional development" for me.

Thank you to my dear friend Brandi Sperry, whose batches of feedback and editing were like much desired Christmas gifts over and over and who looked me in the eye and said, "You do talk about the past less." I tell my students that, whenever they wonder why they should reflect, and no other statement by a friend has ever helped me heal so much.

Thanks to my friend Mark Janzen for telling me "Sometimes I think, if God exists, he manifests primarily as a DJ." That was a good one. I think about that all the time.

Thank you to my posse of best friends: Ann—I love you so much, I don't even have to like your music. Tamiko—we did it: our own private MFA! Victoria, thank you for taking every part of me seriously and knowing when to toast. Elena, I know—I'm sorry I didn't include any Prince in this book, but his spirit and yours are in this book. Laura Cady, thank you for being the biggest female music fan with me and a big fan of me. And to Gretchen, my dance and concert and life partner forever.

186

To my mother Pamela, my sister Amber, my niece Allison, I will listen to anything you play in the car, even if it's Pink!, because I am so grateful for all the singing and dancing. Thank you for being in my family band. (Mom, I know you want us to shut it off—we just can't.)

And all the rest of the love I have, in all the years left, to my husband, Rick, who didn't realize on that couch I'd be emailing him a battery of fully finished essays on love as courtship offerings. Thank you for asking me out before I left and thank you for each morning and night and afternoon and album and song.

Works Cited and References

Abdurraqib, Hanif. "Under Half-Lit Fluorescents: The Wonder Years and the Great Suburban Narrative." *They Can't Kill Us Until They Kill Us*. Two Dollar Radio, 2018. 59-64.

Animal Collective. "Did You See the Words Today." *Feels*. Fat Cat Records, 2005.

Amos, Tori. "Father Lucifer." *Boys for Pele*. Atlantic Records, 1996.

Arcade Fire, The. "Here Comes the Night Time." *Reflektor*. Merge Records, 2013.

Bare, Bobby. "Skip a Rope." *Memphis, Tennessee*. RCA, 1969. Beatles, The. "Something." *Broken Social Scene*. Arts and Crafts, 2004. Beck. "Lost Cause." *Sea Change*. Geffen Records, 2002.

Bush, Kate. "Running Up That Hill." *Hounds of Love*. EMI, 1985. Car Seat Headrest. *Teens of Style*. Matador, 2015.

Clapton, Eric. "Layla." *Layla and Other Assorted Love Songs*. Atco Records, 1970.

Costa, Nikka. "Everybody Got Their Something." *Everybody Got Their Something*. Virgin Records, 2001.

Depeche Mode. "Enjoy the Silence." *Violator*. Mute Records, 1990.

Devo. "Time Out for Fun." *Freedom of Choice*. Warner Bros. Records, 1980.

Doves. "There Goes the Fear." *The Last Broadcast*. Catch and Release Records, 2005.

Dylan, Bob. "Tangled Up in Blue." *Blood on the Tracks*. Columbia Records, 1975.

-----. "Ballad of a Thin Man." *Highway 61 Revisited*. Columbia Records, 1965.

Ellington, Duke. "Fleurette Africaine." *Money Jungle*. United Jazz Artists, 1963.

Fleetwood Mac. "Big Love." *Tango in the Night.* Warner Bros. 1987.

Grizzly Bear. "Two Weeks." *Veckatimst.* Warp, 2009.

Harvey, P.J. "One Line". *Songs from the City, Songs from the Sea.* Island Records, 2000.

Jamison, Leslie. "*The Empathy Exams.*" Greywolf P, 2014.

Juliana Hatfield Three, The. "Spin the Bottle." *Become What You Are.* Mammoth Records, 1993.

Johnson, Eric. "Forty Mile Town." *Ah Via Musicom.* Capitol Records, 1990.

Kings of Convenience. "I Don't Know What I Can Save You From." *Versus* Astralwerks, 2001.

Kishi Bashi. "I Am the Antichrist to You." *151a.* Joyful Noise Recordings, 2012.

Olsen, Angel. *Burn Your Fire for No Witness.* Jagjaguwar Records, 2014.

Other Lives. *Rituals.* TBD Records, 2015.

Phair, Liz. "Cinco de Mayo." *Whip Smart.* Matador, 1994.

Redding, Otis. "These Arms of Mine." *Pain in My Heart.* Stax/Volt, 1962.

Simpkins, Kelsey. "Album Review—Other Lives." beardedgentlemenmusic. 6 May 2016.

Smiths, The. "How Soon Is Now?" *Hatful of Hollow.* Rough Trade, 1985.

Sundays, The. "Love." *Blind.* Parlophone, 1992.

Teenage Fanclub. "Ain't That Enough" and "The Concept." *Songs from Northern Britain.* Creation, 1997.

Tegan and Sara. "Where Does the Good Go?" *So Jealous.* Vapor, 2004.

Van Etten, Sharon. "Jupiter 4." *Remind Me Tomorrow.* Jagjaguwar, 2019.

Zoladz, Lindsay. *Burn Your Fire for No Witness.* Album review. *Pitchfork* Feb. 17, 2014.

Wolf, Kate. "Cornflower Blue." *Give Yourself to Love*. Rhino Entertainment, 1983.

Zoldadz, Lindsay. "Angel Olsen: Burn Your Fire for No Witness." *Pitchfork*, 17 February 2014.

Acknowledgments of Previous Publication

I offer my gratitude to the following publications, in which several of these essays first appeared:

3Elements Review, "Paint It Blacker"

The Bookends Review: "Message in a Bottle"

Carcosa Magazine: "Devo Made My Sister Cool"

HCE Review, "One Line"

Rappahannock Review, "Sound and Vision: There Goes the Fear"

Superstition Review, "Divorce Closet"

"What to Save" was a finalist for the 2021 Porch Prize in Creative Nonfiction